BUILDING DIGITAL PRODUCTS

2ND EDITION

ALEX MITCHELL

DEDICATION

A sincere thank you to my wife Meagan Mitchell for being
the toughest alpha tester I have ever met.

CONTENTS

2ND EDITION INTRODUCTION

It's hard to believe it has been 4 years since I wrote **Building Digital Products**. Over these 4 years, thousands of current and aspiring Product Managers have read this book to help them find their foundation, to level up their Product toolkit, and to help their Product teams and companies be more successful.

I'm still in awe that each and every day someone is reading **Building Digital Products** and sharing their feedback with me. 4 years ago, this was my dream. I'm humbled each day that I get to live this dream and meet new Product Managers around the world.

A lot has changed in 4 years. First, there are now an incredible number of impressive resources for new Product Managers. From page-turning newer Product books like Hooked and Contagious to the Product School, a place specifically built to train and level-up Product Managers, it's been incredible watching the growth of this profession from the inside.

I've changed as well. 4 years ago, I was a relatively new Product Manager at Vistaprint Digital, in way over my head, and trying to learn as much as possible from more senior Product Managers. Over the past 4 years, I've gained significant startup Product experience at Upside Travel and ICX Media, where I currently serve as the Chief Product Officer. Additionally, I've learned an incredible amount as the Founding Advisor of Bullseye, a new EdTech startup I've been helping get off the ground. While the seniority of the Product roles and the companies have changed, I still feel like I'm over my head many days and I'm still trying to learn as much as possible. Some things never change :)

Finally, in addition to updating this book with new stories and new lessons, I've released a new book for a more broad audience than

Building Digital Products. My new book, **Disrupting Yourself**, is a guide on how to succeed in the New Economy. A New Economy where disruption is the new normal, continuous learning isn't optional, and rapid change and adaptation is the only way to survive. **Disrupting Yourself** will help you advance in your career, gain control over your life, build a stronger network than ever before, master continuous learning, build a recognizable brand, and diversify your skills and income. If you enjoy this book (even if you don't!) I'm confident **Disrupting Yourself** will help you achieve more in your life.

I sincerely hope you enjoy this updated version of **Building Digital Products**. I'd love to hear your feedback on Twitter at @amitch5903.

Thank you for reading,
Alex Mitchell

ORIGINAL INTRODUCTION

There is no formula to create the perfect Product Manager.

If you're looking for the exact steps to become the next Steve Jobs, Elon Musk, Chris Cox, or Sundar Pichai, you won't find them in *Building Digital Products*. Also, if you only know two of the four names from the previous sentence, don't worry, there's plenty of time to learn and improve your product knowledge.

What you will find in *Building Digital Products* are three things:

1. **Ideas** (and plenty of them). You'll find ideas for building stronger teams, measuring the right performance metrics, and ideas on how to take your new product through your specific development cycle successfully.

2. **Insights**. Although I'm still relatively new to Product Management, I've distilled the collective wisdom and experiences of my colleagues across many companies into this book. Learn from their mistakes and find success more quickly then they (and I) did. *Building Digital Products* is the book **I wish** I had when I became a Product Manager.

3. **Motivation**. You can be better. Every single day you should be looking to be better. They day you start feeling comfortable with where you are is the day you get stuck. The people who change the world are those who never think they are good enough. Sure, they celebrate the victories in life, but they continually set their sights higher.

So what exactly is a Product Manager?

At the most basic level, a Product Manager is responsible for a product, product group, or delivering on a strategic goal. Product Managers typically work with developers and designers to translate their product vision into discrete tasks that can deliver value to customers.

What does a typical Product Manager look like?

One of the most interesting aspects of the Product Manager position is that people with very different backgrounds can succeed in very different ways.

For that specific reason, I'd like to share some of the more common Product Manager archetypes I've observed.

Please note, this is by no means an exhaustive list and Product Managers come in many, many, forms.

THE TECHNICAL PRODUCT MANAGER (TPM)

The Technical Product Manager almost always was a developer before they moved to product. They also weren't just a developer, they were one of your best developers. Even more, as a developer, they understood what could be shipped quick and dirty and what was worth investing significantly more development time on. They had the Product Manager's instinct even before moving to product.

The Technical Product Manager is an incredible asset for every product team. What they may lack in strategic insights or marketing aptitude, they make up for with their ability to build strong relationships with developers and maximize team output.

Most Often Found at Companies Like: Google, Microsoft, Amazon (AWS), PagerDuty, Cybersecurity, DevOps Companies

THE ANALYTIC/DATA SCIENCE PRODUCT MANAGER (APM)

The Analytic Product Manager is a close cousin of the Technical Product Manager. Additionally, there is a large amount of overlap between the two archetypes. While the TPM was almost always a developer prior to entering product, the APM was almost always an analyst before moving to product. Again, not just a simple analyst, but the strongest analyst your company has. They not only were experts at SQL, Python, or Multivariate Testing, but they understood the power of their recommendations to influence business decisions.

Being an APM/GSD-PM myself, I can share that most APMs find themselves frustrated in only being able to recommend product decisions. They move to product in order to move beyond the simple recommendation to the actual execution of business changing decisions.

The APM is typically the most informed Product Manager about the performance of their products and the other products of the company. They love data and can never get enough.

Most Often Found at Companies Like: Palantir, Looker, Plaid, ML-Heavy Companies

THE MARKETING PRODUCT MANAGER (MPM)

The Marketing Product Manager has an innate understanding of the end customer. They know their customers goals, their personas, and their purchase motivations. Often, MPMs have a background in advertising, PR, or other marketing fields. It's incredibly clear to the MPM which features will sell the product and which ones are irrelevant. They're also cognizant of the power of marketing and how it can make product strengths appear larger and product weaknesses seem non-existent.

The MPM is an essential member of the product team throughout the launch cycle as a new product is brought to market. They'll help with positioning, pricing, and targeting in a way that no other Product Manager can.

Most Often Found at Companies Like: Intercom, Hubspot, Toast, Allbirds

THE "GET SHIT DONE" PRODUCT MANAGER (GSD-PM)

The Get Shit Done Product Manager is an interesting variation on the Product Manager that is much more rare than the TPM, APM, or MPM. The GSD-PM is a hard charger, they don't take no for an answer, and are intensely focused on delivery at all costs. This Product Manager may burn bridges, make enemies, and work their development team to the brink, but they'll achieve their goals.

There isn't room for a GSD Product Manager at every company. For the above reasons, this type of Product Manager is often only found at high growth/high intensity startups and still hard-charging, late-stage, private companies.

Most Often Found at Companies Like: Lime, Bird, Uber (Kalanick era), Facebook (Early Years)

THE VISIONARY PRODUCT MANAGER (VPM)

The Visionary Product Manager is the rarest variety of Product Manager. The VPM positions themselves above the day to day tactical execution that most other Product Managers are consumed by.

They have an innate understanding of their company, of the market, of their customers, and potential customers.

Many VPMs were founders of startups or work at venture capital companies. They think in three year timelines instead of three months. They aren't focused on just this product release, but how it impacts the vision their have for the company in five years.

Most Often Found As: Founders of Seed Stage Startups

What type of Product Manager are you?

Even if you don't fit into one of these major Product Manager archetypes, that's completely fine. I'm confident you will find value in the ideas, insights, and motivation shared in *Building Digital Products*.

Thank you again for selecting this book and let's get to work!

1. IDENTIFY AND UNDERSTAND THE PROBLEM

"The way to get started is to quit talking and start doing"

-Walt Disney

So you're a Product Manager.

Maybe you fell into a role that someone else at your company left, maybe you grew into this position of greater responsibility, maybe you even fit into one of the archetypes of a Product Manager shared in the introduction. Well it's time to get past your self-discovery and move onto your first big test as a Product Manager: Identifying the problem you want to solve.

However, before you get there, let's take a deeper look at the company where you're working:

What stage is your company in?

Are you pre-funding, seed stage, Series A/B, post-acquisition, public, or some financial position that even you don't understand? It's essential to know how much money your company has, where that money comes from, and who you'll be pitching your ideas to.

What are your company's strengths and weaknesses?

Make a quick judgment call.

If one part of your company was going to win a prestigious award, which one would it be?

If you were going to completely divest another, who would you cut loose?

It's a tough decision to make, but so is the world of the Product Manager and you will have to make decisions like this every day. Knowing your organization's strengths and weaknesses will help you build a strong foundation with your product.

What resources (mainly developers and designers) do you have at your disposal?

Even the best Product Manager is lost without developers and designers.

It's important to take inventory of what resources your company has a surplus of and what resources they have severe shortages of. At this point, you shouldn't be too concerned about the exact people you need for your team and their project (we'll cover that in Chapter 4), you should be more focused on understanding areas with strong and weak talent pools in your company.

What tolerance does your company have for failure and development without tangible results?

This assessment is incredibly important and, unfortunately, very difficult to determine in a new role.

You can't simply ask your boss or your investors this question and expect to get an honest answer. However, you can study past projects that were perceived to be "fast" or "slow", "successful" or "disastrous" and start putting together the pieces of the puzzle to measure your company's overall risk tolerance. Before you commit to build a new product or improve a current product, you should know your company's failure threshold.

Is there a bias towards new product development or feature improvement of current products?

The smaller your company, the higher likelihood that you'll skew to "new product bias". The more established your business is, the higher chance that you'll be biased towards incremental features and improvements. There's nothing wrong with these biases; in fact, they're established for very logical reasons. Smaller companies are still looking for their "big product", their major traction or product/market fit, while bigger companies are often looking to maintain their competitive position and keep current customers happy.

IMPROVING EXISTING PRODUCTS

After a thorough evaluation of your company, you've decided to improve your existing products. (If you're only interested in new product development, skip to the second half of this chapter).

Now which product should you focus on improving?

There are several ways to filter your stable of products (assuming you have more than one) to find the most attractive opportunities. One of my favorite techniques is to locate the worst product you sell and explore all of the reasons it's awful.

If you don't think you have any bad products, you are only fooling yourself. Even Apple had the Newton PDA.

How can you use data to find the worst product? Listen to your customers.

Look for the product with the lowest Net Promoter Score (NPS), the lowest engagement rates, and the highest churn.

Not familiar with **Net Promoter Score (NPS)**? Don't worry! We'll cover it in **Chapter 8.**

Another easy way to find this "detractor" product: Ask your support team.

I personally guarantee that your support group will name the product that keeps them up at night, the product that gives them high blood pressure, and the product that is responsible for tons of wasted energy – before you can even get the words out of your mouth.

> *"Great, so I just find the worst product that we offer and that will be the one I work on, right?"*

Wrong! Just because a product is completely awful today doesn't mean it's worth saving. Once you've identified your worst product, you should consider the cost of shutting it down from both a development and financial perspective.

Don't worry about getting the values perfect, rather, focus on the *significant cost* that this product is having on your support group, your development resources, and the reputation of your company. If you judge your worst product is worth saving, what's next? Ask yourself these questions:

1. Can you get excited about fixing the problems with the product?
2. Can you get a team and your company excited about fixing these problems?

If not, shut down the product and find something else to work on.

If you're up for the challenge, it's time to buckle up and jump to Chapter 2, where we'll learn how to ideate ways to solve the key customer problem your product addresses.

CONSIDERING NEW PRODUCT CONCEPTS AND PROBLEMS TO SOLVE

Successful product development arises from a deep understanding of a problem. Often, this is a problem that the Product Manager can deeply empathize with.

What are five problems that you experience in your day to day life that you wish were solved by someone? Having trouble thinking of five? Here are mine to jumpstart your creativity:

1. It took far **too long for me to travel** to my nighttime MBA classes (>45 minutes), which reduced the amount of time I got to spend at home after work and the time I got to sleep.

2. As a Product Manager, I have **10 different tabs open in my chrome browser** to track news, web analytics, A/B testing results, and chat. I really would like all of these in one dashboard.

3. **Hiring new developers takes too long.** I would love to have an automated way to review candidates, test their technical knowledge, bring them onsite, and click one button to extend an offer. If accepted, I want all the necessary paperwork taken care of, so all I need to worry about is the start date and welcoming them to the team. I want the experience of in-house HR/Recruiting without the cost.

4. **Many of the meetings I have are inefficient.** I want an easy, fast, anonymous way to provide instant, effortless feedback on meetings so they either get better or I stop attending. For example, maybe in the future I'll only accept meetings if they have a rating of 80% or higher.

5. **I want an easier way to conduct User Testing**. When I was at Vistaprint Digital, we brought users of our Pagemodo and Vistaprint Social Media Marketing products into the office. However, in order to do that, I had to send an average of five emails per customer, reserve conference rooms, notify building security, and purchase gift cards to compensate users for their time. This is clearly very inefficient. I'd like to use a Slack command to request users for testing with a simple message: "@usertesting need 5 users for 2/5/20".

Find the problems you are passionate about solving. What problems overlap with the areas that your business operates in? A successful product is built with a simple equation:

Pervasive Problem + Product Manager Obsession +
The Right Team = Successful Product

You should focus on solving a very painful issue that affects a large population. Also look for an issue with a solution that is "must-have" and not just "nice-to-have".

Research says that your solution to a problem has to be 10 times better than what's available in the market to be successful. Any less of an improvement and people just won't bother spending the energy to overcome the inertia that's keeping them solving the problem the way they are today.

WHAT DOES 10X IMPROVEMENT LOOK LIKE?

Think Google vs. manually looking up answers in an encyclopedia or Uber vs. searching for a cab company in the yellow pages or even creating a website with a website builder vs. writing your own

HTML, Javascript, and CSS. These are pretty extreme examples, but new product development should be just that: solving big problems in new ways that lead to extremely improved outcomes for customers.

As you're thinking about solving new problems that you and your team are passionate about, it's important to understand how this work will affect your existing products:

- If you're able to solve this problem, will this cannibalize your current product sales or support them?
- Will solving this problem offer additional value to your current customers or not affect them?
- Are you ok with these impacts? Are your stakeholders (managers, investors) ok with them?

It's easy to get excited about new problems to solve because there are many more variables in play and the likelihood of dramatic business changing results is perceived as much greater.

However, the probability of failure is also significantly greater with new product development. As such, your default perspective on new product development should be cynical. You should have to fight to prove that solving a key user problem is valuable.

One of my favorite quotes about new features and new products comes from the site UserTesting.com:

"Feature requests are worthless until proven valuable"

Make sure that your excitement for new product development doesn't cause you to lose perspective on what's essential and what's just interesting or requested often by current customers.

How Are People Solving This Problem Today?

After you've identified the key problems and solutions that you're interested in pitching to your management team, you should research how people are solving this issue today. Talk with real people experiencing this issue and sympathize with the problem even if you can't fully empathize with it yourself.

People will naturally find the lowest-friction method *widely available* to solve the problems that they encounter. However, these *widely available* solutions often **still suck**.

> *How long did people put up with cabs before Uber destroyed the industry?*
>
> *How long did people simply "deal" with calling restaurants for delivery before Grubhub, DoorDash, and Uber Eats brought thousands of restaurants to your door?*

With each of the problems that you explore you should consider: How much does it "cost" people to solve this problem today? Add together the time they spend, the money they pay, and the overall aggravation of the market's current solution to the problem.

Would this same population be willing or able to pay this cost for a solution? Is that purchase price and total addressable market (TAM) attractive to your company at its current stage?

It's also worth noting that some problems are a small nuisance, something to be dealt with on an infrequent basis, resulting in a small additional expenditure of energy. Others are frequent, persistent, and consume a significant amount of time and energy. Which is yours?

It is not complex: you want to solve problems with **high cost, high frequency, and high persistence**.

A **Bad Product Manager** lets others choose what he/she should build next.

A **Good Product Manager** tries to understand the opportunity in both new product ideas and improving existing products periodically.

A **Great Product Manager** is constantly evaluating the biggest opportunities available and also understands how those ideas do or don't fit into the current company climate, developer skill-sets, and his or her own interests and passions.

2. IDEATE TO SOLVE THE PROBLEM

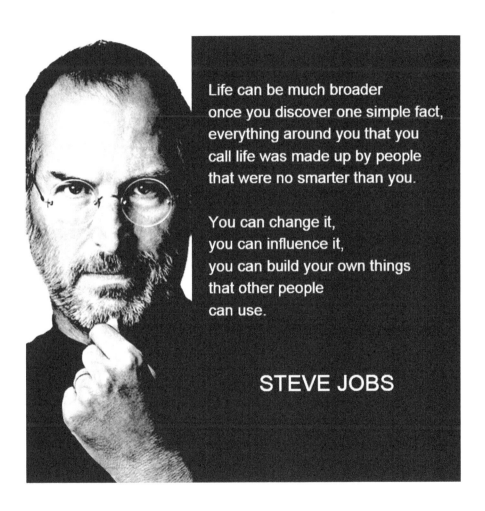

Life can be much broader
once you discover one simple fact,
everything around you that you
call life was made up by people
that were no smarter than you.

You can change it,
you can influence it,
you can build your own things
that other people
can use.

STEVE JOBS

You began your Product Manager journey in the first chapter by deciding to either build something new or to improve an existing product. After making that fundamental decision and identifying the core problem in either case to solve, you now need to ideate on potential solutions to that issue.

Start by mapping the biggest potential solution set; ignore technological and developer limitations. Give yourself at least an hour for this exercise and make sure you have plenty of whiteboard.

*What would an **ideal** solution look like to this problem?*

What if you had to cut 50% of the features from the ideal solution; which could you live without?

Does your problem break down into smaller problems that each have some independent value to customers?

Overwhelmed already?

Check out the easy-to-follow **Ideation checklist** in the supplemental section at the end of the book.

WHO ELSE GETS INVOLVED WITH IDEATION?

At the end of the day, the Product Manager holds the decision rights on how to solve the problem. However, this creative and formative stage is the best opportunity you have to include diverse thinkers from across your organization. Make sure you have as varied of a group as possible.

At this stage, however, it's in your best interest to avoid including doubters, skeptics, or overly-detail-focused individuals. Also, don't eliminate any potential solutions at this stage; your goal is to cast as wide of a solution net as possible.

Need more specifics on how to get started?

Ideally, you should include at least 1 developer, 1 designer, and 1 marketer to provide a broad perspective. Product will still typically drive these creative sessions, but great ideas can come from any-where. Also, consider the motivations of the individuals you invite to participate. Founders, early employees, and Product Managers often have the highest incentives to find solutions, and therefore are the most likely to brainstorm successfully.

Also, leave the computers and smartphones at your desk. Although ideation involves a lot of down-time and thought, these devices are too big of a distraction to keep you connected to the day-to-day noise of your company.

While you are searching for diverse opinions, don't let your ideation group grow too large. Definitely avoid including *secondary* groups like support, legal, or leadership. If you do, you'll likely get paralyzed by trying to overcome implementation, migration, and product consistency issues before you're even found potential solutions. Remember, this is your time to focus on the key user issue and solving it in any way possible, not to make everyone happy.

HOW LONG SHOULD IDEATION BE?

The ideal length of your ideation session depends on the size of your company, the size of the problem, and the quality of the discussion.

Don't be afraid to spend a full day (or even two!) working on ideation if your sessions are productive, the problem is important, and your group remains motivated. If you sense the group energy is decreasing, it's your job as the Product Manager to motivate or end the session.

After you've collected what you judge to be a suitable solution set, make sure to thank everyone who participated. Most importantly, don't make any promises to pursue any of the proposed solutions.

As the Product Manager, you're a decision maker,
not a consensus builder.

The Product Manager controls the decision on what will be built. Your team owns *most* of the decision on how the problem will be solved. "Most" because the Product Manager still has the ability to select between multiple build paths and to determine how much time there is to validate your key hypotheses.

In evaluating potential solutions, it's completely acceptable to acknowledge or pursue solutions that don't completely solve the problem. Rather, you should simply want to solve *enough* of the problem to offer value much greater than the current "cost" experienced by potential users. Additionally, each *part* of the problem you solve is one more point of validation that helps you justify pursuing a more complete solution.

INCREMENTAL PROBLEM SOLVING IS A BETTER APPROACH

1. Uber started as just a **black car company** before disrupting the entire taxi industry. They saw that there was enough of

an opportunity to reduce the "cost" to black cab users to tackle this problem first.

2. Vistaprint began by selling **business cards only** before expanding to offer virtually all print products a small business for marketing.

3. Amazon was founded in 1994 as an **online bookstore only** before expanding years later to offer other products.

4. Webvan, a grocery delivery company that raised close to $1 billion from investors, failed due to its poorly planned rapid expansion, while **Instacart has succeeded** in the same industry years later by expanding geographically only after proving its financial model.

It's also possible that in your ideation sessions, you've found solutions that expand beyond the borders of your company. If this is the case, consider potential partnership or outsourcing opportunities that could bring these solutions to testable reality sooner.

A Product Manager is always responsible for finding the lowest friction and lowest effort way to test his or her hypothesis. Prepare yourself: the lowest friction and lowest effort way will likely still be **damn hard.**

CONSIDERING COMPETITORS

After you and your team have exhausted 90% of your time and 90% of your energy on brainstorming, it's now time to discuss competitor tactics and competitor products. If you consider competitors and the potential solutions they offer any earlier, you'll probably find that many of your team's ideas are simply byproducts of the solutions your competitors have already created.

You may find that no competitors are actually solving this issue today or at least not in the way you imagine an ideal solution. If that is the case, consider:

Why aren't competitors trying to solve this problem?

Are they too busy or have they recognized something that you haven't?

What puts you in a better position to solve this problem than your competitors?

Could they copy your idea easily?

If your competitors are trying to solve this problem, evaluate their success.

Consider what portion of the addressable market they may be serving and any publicly available feedback from their customers. Use their product: what do you like, what don't you like?

At this point, you're well on your way to building. You've identified and understood the problem you want to solve. You've ideated on the potential solutions to that problem. You've built a strong understanding of how your customers and your competitors are or aren't attempting to solve that problem today. Now, it's time to sell your solution.

A **Bad Product Manager** copies his competitors or settles on the first possible "consensus" solution to a problem.

A **Good Product Manager** works to understand the potential solution set from brainstorm sessions and then selects the idea most likely to succeed based on quantitative and qualitative criteria.

A **Great Product Manager** is always collecting information. He/She takes all inputs of data from competitors, customers, teammates, the market, and aggregates this information into a strong position on how this problem should be solved. They welcome input from others, but in the end they make the decision themselves, and don't rely on consensus opinion or majority vote.

As a Product Manager, you'll quickly find that your selling talent can be your biggest asset or your biggest liability. Each and every day, you'll find yourself selling a vision to your team, selling early traction numbers to potential investors, or selling your team and your company to the best developers at another technology startup.

While this book certainly isn't designed to be a manual on sales, it's incredibly important to acknowledge the role that sales plays throughout the product development process.

Once you've identified the problem you want to solve and the way that you want to test to solve it, it's time to build your elevator pitch.

First, figure out **how much time you need** to validate your hypothesis.

Regardless of the size of your company (Seed/Series A/Public/ Private), you're always going to feel pressure to validate hypotheses earlier. Try to find the most lightweight way you can sell your solution to your management team. You need to balance the "wow" factor of your idea with the time to build the solution and the time to realize whether it is a success or failure with a population you care about.

If you need help with best practices on communication with your superiors, give Paul Jackson's guide on "managing upward" a read: A Product Manager's Guide to Managing Upward. Even if you've sold to all types of stakeholders before, Paul's humorous take on Product Management at a *grown digital company* is worth a quick read.

Want daily, tweet-sized, tips on how to sell better?

Check out Steli Efti's newsletter at Close.io

THE RIGHT AND WRONG WAYS TO COMMUNICATE DATES

Once you've figured out your internal estimate of how long it will take to validate your hypothesis, what dates do you choose to communicate with leadership or investors? As the Product Manager, you need to be extremely careful about the dates that you communicate. As soon as a date leaves your lips, you may as well carve it onto a stone tablet and hang it around your neck. Don't forget these wise words from Paul Jackson:

"Until you ship, communication is the deliverable."

No qualifications or confidence intervals can solve for the fact that management and investors will hear the earliest date you mention and assume the product will be delivered by then, if not sooner. A great Product Manager communicates dates only when absolutely necessary and is careful not to commit to key features associated with those dates. The product building process is a very fluid one and the nature of your solution may *will definitely* change as you build.

Regardless of the dates you choose to communicate, you should aim to show value as fast as you can with a MVP and "earn value later". Never forget that you are fighting to validate a hypothesis as quickly as possible.

Ask these questions (and many more):

1. *Will our current users pay more for this feature?*

2. *Will new visitors to our website purchase this product?*

3. *Does this product or service result in lower churn and higher engagement for current customers?*

SPEED TO VALUE ABOVE ALL ELSE

With your MVP, you are trying to show value **as quickly as possible** to your stakeholders. Yes, I already said this, but I can't possibly say it enough: **speed to value above all else**. "Value" in this context means increased engagement, NPS, or tangible conversion rate/bookings/ other financial impact.

Even if the way you extract this value isn't fully sustainable, that's ok! You can fully realize or productionalize this value later with a more robust build out after you've earned the time to complete the product the "right way". It's important to understand I'm not advocating taking shortcuts that will damage a future product, only those decisions that can be made today without negatively impacting tomorrow.

STAY FOCUSED WITH YOUR PRODUCT PITCH

Keep your focus on the core problem/solution pair and absolutely crush it. In your pitch, just like your eventual development, you need to stay focused. Scope and feature creep are the biggest killers of successful product development. In this initial build out, it's your job to keep your team (and yourself) laser-focused on the core problem and the core solution you're pursuing and destroy that first before tackling anything else. Your pitch should be laser-focused as well.

It's incredibly tempting along the way to solve other problems that you see and, trust me; you'll see plenty of other problems. However, if you don't stay focused, you'll end up solving no problems well enough, and you'll be left with a product that is just as unfocused in appearance to your customers as the development process was to you and your team. I've made this mistake before and it's a devastating one!

WHERE'S THE VALUE?

In selling your solution, make sure to share the potential value your solution will generate.

Unless you're at Kiva (well actually, even if you are at Kiva), eventual value is the most important aspect of your solution to stakeholders. If you found a solution to a frequent problem that affects a large number of people who aren't willing to pay it, you've found nothing. If you found a great solution to a problem that affects a very small population, you've found nothing. If you found a solution to a problem that affects a large number of people who are willing to pay for that solution, you may have found something.

Everyone can think of the major, but highly infrequent, exceptions to this value-pursuant rule: WhatsApp, Snapchat, TikTok, Instagram, and several other big name technology companies. However, it's unlikely that you'll have this luxury as a Product Manager, especially if you are a first-time one. Even the Product Managers at these companies thought about ways to monetize their products, even if they chose ultimately not to pursue them for many years.

SELLING THE SOLUTION TO THE CUSTOMER

Part of any product development process for both new and existing products is thinking about how to sell this new solution to customers. As the Product Manager, it's your job to help make this problem extremely tangible to those experiencing it and to advertise your new and better solution in a compelling way.

For example, as I write this, I'm looking out of the window at a D.C. public bus with a massive Lyft banner on it. This banner is a constant reminder that the status-quo (i.e. taking a 2 hour bus ride to go 5 miles) completely sucks and I should use Lyft instead.

Communication and sales are two of the most important skills you need as a Product Manager. Figure out a reasonable estimate for time-to-value. Communicate fixed dates to management only when necessary. Compellingly sell the long-term vision to your team, your stakeholders, and your customers. Finally, share how you expect to validate your key hypotheses along the way. Now, let's start building the right team.

A **Bad Product Manager** reads off of slides on the pros and cons of a new product or incremental product improvement.

A **Good Product Manager** starts from a problem-focus and builds towards a plan for a potential solution to that problem. They share what they will measure to validate their hypotheses.

A **Great Product Manager** commands their audience. He/She starts with a problem and makes it so palpable that it's all you can think about. They make you starved for a solution and then over-deliver on that desire with an answer so clear that you can't believe you didn't think of yourself. They clearly share the next steps on how they will build their team, how they will recognize success, and what the "new-world" looks like with their product in it.

4. BUILD THE RIGHT TEAM THE FIRST TIME

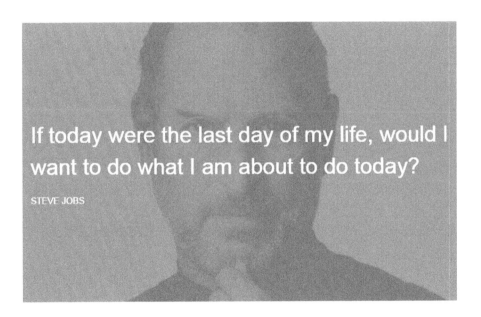

If today were the last day of my life, would I want to do what I am about to do today?

STEVE JOBS

60% of total team effectiveness comes from team design (Hackman, Organizing Agile Teams). This means that only 40% of your success comes from team launch, planning, motivation, nature of work, and other factors. Crazy, right?

So, even if you identify the perfect problem, you are passionate about tackling it, and you sold it beautifully to your organization, you're likely to fail miserably without the right people on the right team with the right structure.

Who should you "hire" or bring onto your team?

Don't Have Hiring Rights?

As the Product Manager, you are the *CEO of your product*. Even if you don't have formal hiring rights for your product team, you should have a very powerful voice in all hiring decisions.

First, you should look for a mixture of technical skill-sets. It's incredibly important to have as varied of technological backgrounds as possible so that you aren't forced to rely on other teams or outsource.

This variety not only includes a mix of front-end/back-end or programming language expertise, but also a balance of age and experience. This diversity will help you through the different parts of the development process and provide you a wide range of perspectives. Younger or less experienced members of the team often tend to be more creative and more risk-taking, while older or more experienced team members have likely built and launched several products.

They know the key risks to look for because they've been burnt before.

Although you're looking for varying technical skill-sets, ages, and career experience, you absolutely need compatible personalities. You need to have a "one tribe" mentality. You need to share the same key values to work together effectively.

WHAT VALUES SHOULD MY TEAM SHARE?

Quick Team Exercise: Tape a large rectangle (8 ft. x 3 ft.) on the ground.

Ask each question from the list below and point to a side for each opposing response. Instruct team members to stand where their personal values lie: one end, the other, or somewhere in between.

- Release fast/break things vs. robust testing agenda?
- Commit to master vs. deploy carefully through multiple testing environments?
- Make money vs. grow our free features and user base?
- Build a great product vs. sell our product better than anyone else?
- Team sprint commitment only vs. "20% time" work in every sprint?
- "Morning person" vs. "night person"
- Sprint commitments vs. Kanban

Shared values are essential to your team's success. If you took the best developers from the top 10 tech companies and put them onto a team together, they would most likely *definitely* fail. Egos will clash, technology experience will vary widely, and perspectives on when to release will be dramatically different.

If you can't reach agreement on these key development beliefs in this early, very "theoretical" time period, you need to rebalance your team to be more effective.

This is much harder than it sounds, often requiring transfers, rejections, or even layoffs. But when the code starts getting written, it's incredibly painful, slow, and inefficient to switch team members or to re-orient around new values.

SPEED FOR MVP, PRECISION FOR FULL RELEASE

While it's still important for your team to deliver a quality product for the MVP stage, the team you build should have two gears. One gear (high speed) should move you as quickly as possible to test a hypothesis. In this gear, it's often ok to take on code quality risk as the product won't be exposed to a full-release audience and will likely not have as large of a reputation risk to your business (if that's even a concern at all). The other gear (medium speed) should take your team from the validation of that hypothesis to a full, quality, stable release to a large number of users.

This "gear change" between product stages should not be underestimated. A change in speed also means a change a change in philosophy. In an MVP build, the best Product Managers are driven by a killer focus to validate a hypothesis in the quickest, often dirtiest, way possible. Once that hypothesis has been validated, the team needs to slow down and determine the best way to build that hypothesis validation into a functional product.

> ### Need More Tips to Build the Right Team?
>
> Check out the "Building Teams" Checklist at the end of this book for easy-to-follow steps to build the best possible team.

When we're building the team, how do we know if developers will be compatible without investing months in team building? Check out this tool from Agility Health called the "Team Health Assessment": Team Health Assessment

DEVELOPER MOTIVATION

Do you understand what motivates developers at your company? Is it the desire to write code that reaches a large number of users? Is it writing quality code that will stand the test of time? Or, is it working on a high visibility project that gets a lot of attention at your company?

Make sure your project lines up with the motivations of the developers you recruit. Also, make sure that when you pitch this project to your developers, you use the right language so that they can personally identify with team goals.

What should be outsourced from a development perspective?

For a small organization, outsourcing development is often not a choice, but rather a necessity. However, when you outsource your development, try to avoid outsourcing the key functionality of the product you're building.

For example, don't second guess outsourcing landing pages, marketing messaging, or pricing grids. But you should be hesitant to outsource the parts of your product that are core to validation of your hypotheses.

A **Bad Product Manager** lets others build their team for them (leadership, engineering management, product management) and just deals with it.

A **Good Product Manager** is an active participant in their team structure, hiring decisions, skill-sets and personalities.

A **Great Product Manager** spends a significant amount of time thinking about how to structure his/her team and has a deep understanding of what personalities, development skills, and shared values he/she needs to achieve success. A great Product Manager also reacts quickly when they've made incorrect hiring decisions or see team-based issues appear.

5. BUILD VS. BUY

Be stubborn ON VISION BUT FLEXIBLE ON DETAILS

Jeff Bezos

Each and every week, a Product Manager typically makes at least one build vs. buy decision. These choices have the potential to accelerate your testing and development cycles or slow them considerably. You need to choose wisely, each and every time.

Here's a recent sample of some of the build vs. buy decisions I've made:

- Should we build our own Audience Intelligence front-end or leverage a best-in-class visualization solution like Looker, Domo, or Tableau?
- Should we build our own onboarding for our social products or use an onboarding as a service provider?
- Do we want to manage our own iOS app notifications or use a service to manage them for us?
- Could we use a partner to simplify our in-product marketing message delivery or should we construct marketing modals, banners, and emails ourselves?

Since the beginning of the modern service economy, businesses and consumers have had to decide:

Do I want to pay for this service or can/should I do it myself?

Add the other variables to consider of maintainability, scalability, user-friendliness, cost, customization, stability and you've quickly given yourself a migraine.

To keep it simple, there are **10 factors** that you should consider with each and every build vs. buy decision.

1. Is this project related to my team's or my business's focus?

2. How long would this take to Build? How long to Buy and integrate?

3. How much time do I have to launch this product?

4. What timing and knowledge uncertainties are there with each path?

5. What are the user-facing quality differences between Build and Buy?

6. What vendors sell a solution to the problem?

7. Are vendors dependable or small startups likely to shut down?

8. How much does it cost to Buy vs. Build? (Don't forget to value your developer's time!)

9. Does the solution match your business type? (Solutions that are right for an enterprise probably aren't right for your startup.)

10. What's the risk that a bought solution breaks in the future or a built solution needs to re-built?

WHEN SHOULD I ALMOST ALWAYS BUY?

Save yourself a headache by purchasing solutions to problems in these areas.

NON-CORE COMPETENCE

If you're in the business of Social Media Analytics as a Service, don't waste time building out a Customer Management System when there are easy and affordable options like Intercom available.

UNCERTAIN TECHNICAL CHALLENGES

If your team doesn't have any idea how they would solve the problem, don't make them spend days or weeks just trying to figure it out. Bite the bullet, invest in your future, and invest in the solution that someone else has already built.

FEATURE DOESN'T DELIVER HIGHLY VISIBLE VALUE

For problems generally not visible to your users (ex. Server Stability, Click Tracking, Purchase Analytics), you're usually better off going with a purchased solution than building your own. Save yourself time, headaches, and (surprisingly) money by integrating NewRelic or DataDog instead of combing through your server logs every night when something goes wrong.

RAPID PROTOTYPING

If you're trying to validate or test a hypothesis in the market, buying (or even better, free-trialing) a few key products could shorten your time to answers by weeks, if not months.

WHEN SHOULD I ALMOST ALWAYS BUILD?

Building is strongly recommended for core features and when customization is essential.

CORE PRODUCT FEATURES

Don't ever purchase a product as a core product feature (be extremely careful if you do). Even if that product strengthens yours in the short-term, it will be more difficult to maintain, harder to update/remove, and much more expensive in the long term than building it yourself today.

Lightweight and well-maintained APIs are an exception here. These services can be especially valuable for complex core product features like payments and email.

CONTROL AND/OR CUSTOMIZATION ARE VITAL

If design, function, and flexibility are incredibly important in solving a problem, don't fool around with trying to significantly modify a purchased solution into your product. Chances are, even if you can get their solution to meet your strict guidelines, it won't stay that way for long and one update by your provider will force you to re-write all of your CSS.

HOW DO I KNOW WHEN BUYING WAS A FAIL?

So you bought a solution and you're already regretting it. How do you know if you're just experiencing buyer's remorse or if it's time to cancel the contract and get building?

SIGNS OF BUYER FAIL

1. Your developers have spent over 3 days working on CSS styling
2. Every day, you think of 5 new ways that the bought solution could be improved. Yes I know as a Product Manager, this is almost impossible not to do, but you get the point!
3. Every month when you pay your subscription bill, you regret it.
4. The bought solution doesn't improve each and every month. In other words, the company you're a customer of is not investing in the feature.

HOW DO I KNOW WHEN BUILDING WAS A FAIL?

So you started building a solution and you're regretting it. How do you know if you're just experiencing growing pains or if it's time to buy a solution?

SIGNS OF BUILDING FAIL

1. You find yourself saying this every day: "I can't wait until we get back to ..." This means you and your team aren't working on the most important thing.
2. Your launch plan for the solution doesn't include user testing or user feedback.
3. The first sprint of development work is more than half filled with spikes (discovery) instead of actual development work.

Although you'll find yourself with build vs. buy decisions on a very frequent basis as a Product Manager, that doesn't mean you can take these choices lightly.

If you anchor your new product to the wrong partner or decide to build a feature that could have been easily integrated, you'll find yourself wasting valuable time and often unable to deliver on the solution you intended to test.

A **Bad Product Manager** thinks build vs. buy is an easy decision and uses the same, limited criteria to decide the path forward.

A **Good Product Manager** respects the significance of each build vs. buy decision, understanding the risks, costs, and rewards of each choice before identifying a path forward.

A **Great Product Manager** makes a significant number of build vs. buy decisions, weighing each criterion differently based on the part of the product that this decision affects. They also know the warning signs of Buyer or Builder fail and when to pivot, if necessary, to another option.

6. GATHERING FEEDBACK IN THE BUILD CYCLE

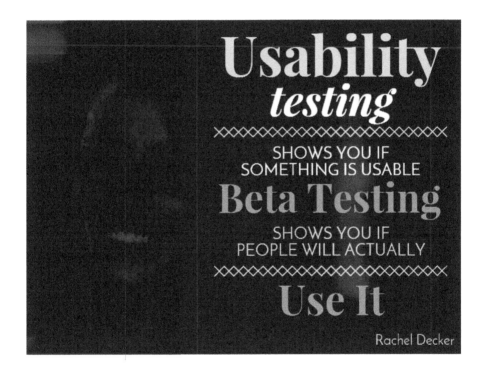

You've built your team. You're educated on build vs. buy decisions. Now, you're ready to start your team coding at a speed they've never coded before. Hold up.

Let's understand how we're going to prototype and test our way through the development cycle before we get too far ahead of ourselves.

Let's start by breaking our mountain of a problem into smaller elements of work called "Epics".

What is an Epic?

An epic captures a large body of work. It is essentially a large user story that can be broken down into a number of smaller tasks. It may take several sprints or weeks to complete an epic. Also, an epic can span more than one project, if multiple projects are included in the board to which the epic belongs.

Those epics break down into smaller pieces we call "User Stories". These are written from a problem-focused perspective, with the end user always in mind. Each user story can be tested independently, delivered independently, and offers tangible value to a user.

What is a Story?

A user story is a tool used to capture a description of a software feature from an end-user perspective. The user story describes the type of user, what they want, and why. A simple example of a user story is: "As a user, I should be able to export my data to a CSV file."

The Product Manager's role in development begins with the writing of user stories and the grouping of these stories into epics that can be accomplished over sprints (typically 2 week periods, but vary by company). Additionally, and most importantly, a Product Manager determines when a story is completed and the priority of that story in the backlog.

What is the Backlog?

The backlog is a collection of user stories, grouped by epic and sorted in descending priority. These priorities are set (and frequently reset) by the Product Manager. Each sprint, the team will select which stories to bring out of the backlog and to commit to complete in a fixed period.

Once the Product Manager has completed their stories and grouped those stories into logical epics, it's time for grooming and estimation. These meetings help the Product Manager attach technical details to user stories, understand the tradeoffs of different technical approaches, and estimate the amount of work each story will take.

What is Estimation?

Estimation is where the development (and testing) team again discuss the (now groomed and polished) user stories. After a brief discussion to refresh everyone's memory, each member of the team selects a "point value" that they believe reflects the amount of work contained in developing, testing, and launching the piece of functionality to users.

This point value does not directly correlate with time to complete the ticket, but rather offers the team, over time, a better idea of how many "points" can be completed in a "sprint". Need an easy solution for online estimation? Check out Bitpoints.io to make estimation a little more fun!

After a Product Manager has written their stories, groomed the details, estimated the complexity, and added those stories to a sprint, code can start being written.

While making it through these ceremonies can feel like a major accomplishment and an opportunity to relax for some Product Managers, it shouldn't be. Re-ordering the backlog, grooming, and estimation, like bathing, are not one time tasks. They require constant tweaking and maintenance to perfect. Many successful teams, my own included, are always looking for ways to make these processes more effective. Have downtime as a Product Manager? Here are some of the things the best Product Managers do with that downtime: How the Best Product Managers Handle Downtime

What is Grooming?

Grooming is an opportunity for the Product Manager to discuss the user stories he or she has created with their development team. The development team should then discuss the technical work and suggest several approaches of differing complexity, time-to-completion, and user impact (if available). The Product Manager then selects which approach to pursue.

As your team begins writing code, it's already time to start thinking about how you plan to test and release. However, before you get there, you'll want to make sure your team is doing code reviews and that you have a strong quality assurance (QA) process.

> ### What are Code Reviews?
>
> Code reviews are an opportunity for other members of the development team to review the code submitted to resolve a user story and offer suggestions on how to improve it. They are vital to the QA process and help diffuse knowledge about particular code to the team.

EVOLUTION OF A FEATURE RELEASE

THE RELEASE STARTS WITH THE TEAM

Each feature should being its testing and release journey within the team. The icons below indicate that this should be the easiest part of feature testing, but it also is extremely high value. You and your team should be experts of the product, know its vulnerabilities, and understand how to test features in the most efficient way possible. This step of a release should also only consume a relatively small piece of time.

Difficulty: ●○○○○

Value: ●●●●○

Time: ●●○○○

What should a Product Manager worry about and look for at this stage of release?

Focus on fixing all of the critical path bugs that would "derail" any rational outside tester. These include issues that destroy the user experience, crash the application, or make it generally unusable.

As the Product Manager, it's your job to motivate your team to live and breathe the product. Make your team want to use the product outside of work, inspire them to want to perfect the experience so much that they choose to work on it on their own time.

It sounds strange to say, but the Product Manager and the team should be the biggest users of the product. This concept is referred to as "dogfooding": the practice of using your own products. You would be amazed at how many development teams I've seen that aren't familiar with many features of their product. If you and your team don't know absolutely everything about your product, you never will reach your full potential.

EXPAND TESTING TO CO-WORKERS

Difficulty: ●●○○○
Value: ●●●○○
Time: ●○○○○

What should a Product Manager worry about and look for at this stage of release?

Be cognizant of different perspectives, different technological abilities, and common pain points. Again, as a Product Manager, you are bombarded with different perspectives, new ideas, and requests to fix issues. It's your role to understand which tasks are worth your team's effort and which are destined for the backlog.

Also, pay attention to what surprises your colleagues.

What features or functionality beat their expectations?

What came in well below their expectations or distracted them from your core features?

A notepad (or Evernote) is your best friend at this stage as you collect a full spectrum of ideas for the product today and the product of the future. In terms of techniques, everything is fair game. Depending on the product and your time, I recommend trying a mixture of paper prototyping, wireframing, design comps, and Figma.

LEARN MORE FROM EXPERTS

Paper Prototyping: http://www.paperprototyping.com/what.html

Wireframing: https://www.youtube.com/watch?v=T0vt3nLZKks

Find out what works best for you and your team or, if you have enough time, try each technique above for the best variety of feedback.

ENGAGE NEARBY BUSINESSES

Difficulty: ●●●○○
Value: ●●●●○
Time: ●●○○○

If you work in a co-working space, nearby companies are an incredible opportunity to test your new product. These people will offer a perspective that is not tainted by your team's unbridled optimism.

Even if you're not in a traditional coworking space, chances are you work close to other companies. Catch people as they go in or out and invite them to test. Sure, you'll feel a little uncomfortable, but the feedback you get will be more than worth it. Difficulty here is higher than with the previous two groups, but so is the value.

USE A TESTING SERVICE (LIKE USERTESTING.COM)

Difficulty: ●○○○○
Value: ●●●○○
Time: ●○○○○

Throughout my career at Vistaprint, Upside, and ICX Media, I've been a big fan of UserTesting.com for one simple reason: it's the fastest way to expose your site/app/idea to a semi-targeted population and get valuable feedback. While it's not free, it is affordable, quick (usually about 1 hour), reliable, and incredibly easy to use.

However, it's also worth noting that there are self-selection biases (the testers are typically savvier than the average member of the population) and appeasement biases (a poor review of my testers could lose them future testing opportunities).

Finally, and most significantly, there is no opportunity to follow-up with reviewers as you make updates to see if improvements change their previous opinions. Even given these drawbacks, testing services have high value in your release cycle.

TEST WITH YOUR TARGET POPULATION

Difficulty: ●●●●○
Value: ●●●●●
Time: ●●●●○

Well, it certainly took a lot of effort, but you've finally worked your way through the release cycle to your "target population". Along the testing journey, you've uncovered bugs, heard feedback from colleagues and nearby coworkers, and maybe even a few online randos (usertesting.com). It's time for the big-leagues; it's time to test with your target users.

Some organizations even have an "always-ready" population for testing new ideas. This is great, but again, you have a self-selecting bias at work here.

Why are people choosing to be part of this population?

What incentives do they receive to participate?

The most reliable way to find your target population is to first determine the key demographics that you want to hear from. If you're working on a new referral program, this could be users who have recently talked about your brand on social media or who have engaged with your company over email.

Start by creating an email list of this population and send a personal appeal to "help us with a new feature/new product test." Surprisingly, no incentive is often needed. Depending on the engagement of your customers and the strength of your relationship, you can expect response rates of 1-5% on an attached, targeted survey.

As the Product Manager hungry for feedback, make sure to follow up personally with everyone who completes your survey. It should be your goal to talk with **at least 50% of these users**.

Figure out how they **felt** as they used your new product or feature, learn about what they wish they could do, what they loved, what they hated. If possible, bring these users in to your office, buy them coffee or lunch, become friends.

These users are a wealth of information waiting to be uncovered. It's not surprising that this is the most difficult and time consuming group to test your new product or feature with. It also shouldn't be surprising, that they are by far the most important.

The build and feature release cycles can be long, but for good reason. There are a lot of moving parts, a number of opportunities to refine your methods of testing hypotheses, and many chances to interact with key user populations that can provide you invaluable feedback.

A **Bad Product Manager** outsources his/her usertesting to a group designated to manage that function.

A **Good Product Manager** tries to understand user behavior on an as-needed or time-permitting basis. They take the findings from these studies and work to implement them in their products.

A **Great Product Manager** always has their finger on the pulse of the user. User testing is not something to schedule or plan for, it's a natural part of every phase of the development lifecycle and they feel naked without it. They don't even need to consciously think about how a customer would perceive a new feature or UI design. They are the customer. They are the user.

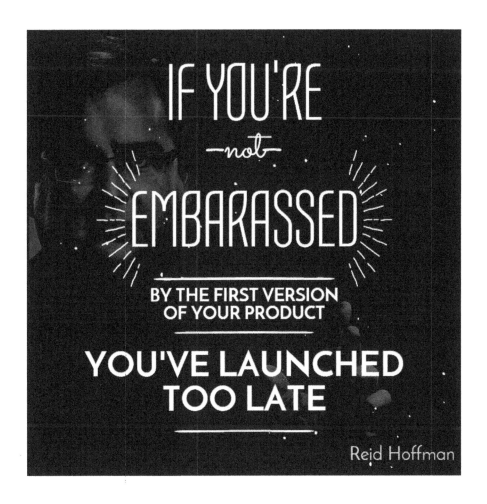

Now that agile development is over two decades old (Wikipedia: Agile Software Development), a significant amount has been written around different philosophies for Minimum Viable Products, Minimum Lovable Products, and Minimum Releasable Products among many, many other conceptual variations of the first version of a product.

Not an expert on these terms? Don't worry, we'll help you understand them better and also discover what type of public release is right for you.

Minimum Viable Product (MVP): The smallest thing we can test to enable one cycle of the build – measure – learn loop. This is the lowest level of product sophistication and likely may appear unpolished. However, this product is viable enough to provide the measurements and learnings that you need to continue development.

Minimum Lovable Product (MLP): The MLP is a solid step above the MVP. An MLP isn't just usable by customers, it's lovable. It's a product or a feature that they would talk to their friends about, one that they would use with a smile on their face. If you care about how your new products impact your existing brand, aim higher for an MLP.

Minimum Releasable Product (MRP): An MRP is another, often very big, step above the MLP. MRP is a more common concept at larger companies where a feature or product can't simply be viable or loveable; it needs to be release-ready from the beginning. For example, a new product or feature at Adobe needs to integrate into the Adobe ecosystem, offer the same single sign-on, and the same billing system. Even if an Adobe product is loveable, that's not enough since they hold themselves to a MRP standard.

If you're looking to dive a little deeper, I especially enjoy writings by these authors:

Jon Pittman: The Tyranny of the Minimum Viable Product

Laurence McCahill: Make Your Minimum Product Loveable

Matt Schlict: The Secret to Designing the Right Product

As always, process the interesting ideas and points made by others, but make sure to use your own judgment as to how to apply the concepts they propose. Your interpretation and use of each of these agile "best-practices" should depend on your industry, your company, your management, your team, and your own personal beliefs.

ALPHA RELEASES

Alpha populations should be opt-in.

Alpha releases should be to people who have willingly indicated that they like your (past) products or company so much that they want to be first in line to test new things, even when your product is far from ready for prime-time.

While some Product Managers often think of Alpha populations as a group of semi-anonymous "users", this population should always include anyone in your personal network that you think can provide valuable feedback.

This means: family, friends, former co-workers, former colleagues, and anyone else you think is up for the challenge. *Why a challenge?* Because at this point, you're trying to gather feedback on a product that may or may not have enough value to truly be worth using.

Your Alpha population may have to push themselves to use the product enough to provide the critical feedback you and your team need.

THE ALPHA COMMUNITY

Your Alpha population should feel like a **community**; a community that you can share half-formed ideas with and get honest feedback from. It's important that you respect and value this feedback whether you choose to act on it or not. If a member of your Alpha population emails you on a Saturday night, email them back right away. Great Alpha users are hard to find and they can often be the difference between the long-term success and failure of your product. If you can expose 90% of the shortcomings of your product during the Alpha release, you'll be in significantly better shape for the Beta and full releases.

WHAT DOES THE PRODUCT LOOK LIKE IN AN ALPHA RELEASE?

An Alpha product typically is very rough around the edges. While it *works*, it may not be supported in all planned use-cases. It may not have features that are very close to "core". It may not be better than other alternatives in the market or even those alternatives offered by your own company. This is ok. You're aiming with the Alpha release to learn about the usability, functionality, and features of what you've built, not its financial viability.

WHAT ARE ACCEPTABLE ALPHA PRODUCT FAILURES?

There are many acceptable Alpha product failures. "Acceptable" meaning that you shouldn't worry if your product fails in these ways during the Alpha release:

- Missing non-core or auxiliary features
- Extra steps required for users to experience the product
- No lifecycle or triggered emails
- Vapor features (meaning non-active, but clicks/data/intent recorded)

WHAT ARE UNACCEPTABLE ALPHA PRODUCT FAILURES?

"Unacceptable" Alpha product failures are unacceptable because they render your product un-useable. Worse than that, these failures make it impossible to get accurate feedback from your Alpha population. Key unacceptable product failures include:

- Significant instability or downtime of the product
- Missing core features
- Product provides no additional value to users

MOST IMPORTANT FEEDBACK IN ALPHA RELEASE

Qualitative. Look for common stumbling blocks that your product causes with users. Filter feedback that reflects features you already plan on building.

For example, if you hear from your Alpha release that your product really needs to post to more social networks than Facebook and you planned on adding more social networks in the Beta release, don't be discouraged! Instead use this as an opportunity to collect even deeper feedback:

What other social networks would you like to post to?

How would you expect to add and remove posting destinations?

Would you expect the experience posting to different social networks to differ from Facebook posting?

Also, it's worth noting that not every product needs a formal Alpha population. There are a few cases where it might be ok to skip Alpha testing and move straight from internal testing to a Beta release:

- Your team completed very robust user testing in your build process (Chapter 6)
- Small startup without an Alpha testing base outside of friends and family
- Excessive time pressure from management

While this final reason is certainly understandable, be careful not to release a product before it provides value. If you do, you run the risk of damaging your brand and distracting yourself and your team with an Alpha population that will be largely unhappy.

BETA RELEASES

Beta releases should expose your product to a small percentage of non-opt-in customers.

As a Product Manager, the beta release is where it **all gets very real**. It's the first time where you truly get to see your product out in the "wild" with users who don't have a selection bias, aren't usually tolerant of any (perceived) missing features or bugs, and may not even be interested in providing you feedback.

MOST IMPORTANT FEEDBACK IN BETA RELEASE

Quantitative. While qualitative feedback is still incredibly important at the Beta stage, the amount of qualitative feedback to sift through (reviews, comments, emails) may be overwhelming in a Beta release making it hard to digest. Look at your stability metrics and your key performance indicators to determine success here.

> Don't know your **KPIs** yet? Don't worry, Chapter 8 will help you determine the most important metrics for your product.

BENEFITS OF RELEASING EARLY

- Fast feedback
- Iterate quicker
- Talk with real users faster
- Collect quantitative data earlier

RISKS OF RELEASING EARLY

- Reputation damage
- Customer churn
- PR release opportunity lost
- Product isn't usable enough to validate hypotheses

Company structure matters a lot when it comes to the timing of Beta releases. If the structure of your company makes it difficult to make updates quickly (ex. intensive strategic planning, long release cycles), you'll probably want to lean more towards a MRP than a MVP. If you can pivot and react to feedback quickly, lean towards an MVP, learn more and move quickly.

Confused on what type of minimum product (Viable, Releasable, Lovable) type you should aim towards releasing?

Consider your company's personality and size, the two primary factors you should consider and use the chart below to help decide what type of product release strategy is right for you. Like everything we've mentioned in this book, the decision is yours and feel free to disagree with the chart!

		Small	Medium	Large
Corporate Personality	Aggressive	MVP	MVP	MVP
	Moderate	MVP	MLP	MLP
	Conservative	MRP	MRP	MRP
		Small	Medium	Large
		Company Size		

65

A **Bad Product Manager** releases every product the same way, because that's "the way we always have done it".

A **Good Product Manager** has focused goals for each release stage and creatively reacts to position his/her product best for each release given available features and overall stability.

A **Great Product Manager** intimately understands their company from both a size and personality perspective. They know what level of polish is appropriate for each release stage and can find the right users to engage for feedback. Even with this knowledge, they're always pushing to release earlier, to learn quicker, and to put their products in customer's hands sooner.

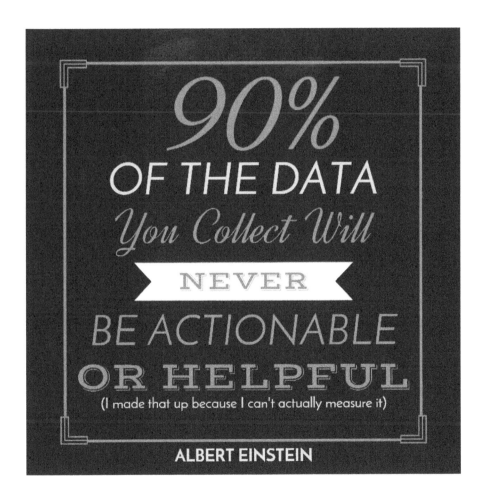

As we discussed in earlier chapters, a successful Product Manager needs to be part salesman, part creative, part team-builder, part motivator, and full-time decision maker.

However, we haven't mentioned that this Product Manager also needs to be a very strong analyst for most companies. The great Product Manager has a keen understanding of what separates trustworthy data from misleading data. It doesn't matter if you've ever written a SQL query (you probably should learn), it doesn't matter if you've never had a passion for discussing the differences between Elastic, BigQuery, and Postgres databases, you still need to be *dangerous with data.*

I'm pretty sick of the term "big data," but today's Product Manager, regardless of company size/vertical/position, needs to acknowledge the competitive landscape of data analysis or get out of the way.

WATCH OUT FOR "VANITY" METRICS

Vanity metrics include statistics like registered users, downloads, and raw pageviews. They are very easily manipulated and typically only move in one direction: up. To a Product Manager, these metrics have very little value. They're great for PR and that's about it.

Everybody knows the Product Manager who only presents these kind of metrics. He/She may even *wow* a few of the more naïve members of you company, but not you. You know that the metrics you really care about are much deeper, much more significant, and that vanity metrics just aren't worth your time.

The worst part about reporting vanity metrics is that you're often forced to continue to report them. If you fail to keep reporting downloads to investors or the press for example, they'll assume the worst. If you keep reporting downloads, you also strongly risk focusing your team on a metric that isn't important. Lose, Lose.

KEY PERFORMANCE INDICATORS AKA "REAL METRICS"

The Key Performance Indicators (KPIs) you choose depend on your type of business and the stage of the growth cycle that you are in. However, a few safe metrics to measure include active users (Daily/Weekly/Monthly), net promoter score (NPS), repeat engagement, cost per acquisition, cohort churn, and publish/key action rate.

Confused about these metrics or want to learn more? Check out the Kiss Metrics Blog for great, in-depth articles about each metric and how to best track them.

Additionally, I'd highly recommend reading **Measure What Matters** by John Doerr to learn about the transformational process of setting Objectives and Key Results (OKRs).

STAY CONNECTED

How closely should you stay connected to the metrics you've selected?

Very closely: Thinking about them as you fall asleep closely. With a new product or new feature, a Product Manager should be consuming as much data as he/she can. Often, in the early days of development, data is unorganized, unfiltered, and, many times, not even available to consume. However, a strong Product Manager interprets data early in the release cycle in order to help uncover which parts of the product or feature are thriving, which are failing miserably, and why.

WHAT SHOULD I MEASURE?

If you're a first time Product Manager, data can be very overwhelming. Between Google Analytics, Heap, SQL queries, Optimizely, and qualitative data sources, you're spending more time trying to access data rather than *getting insights from it*. Simplify your life and start with A-C-E goals.

Choose 3 Key Metrics (A-C-E)

1. AN ACTIVITY METRIC

- What is the key feature of your product?
- What do you want every new user to do?
- What user action makes you throw your hands up in the air and scream "hell yeah!"?

That is your activity metric.

For the website builders on Webs and Vistaprint, the key activity metric is publish rate. At Pagemodo, the key activity metric was the use of our scheduled posts feature for Social Media. At Upside Travel, it was purchasing a 2nd trip with us. Choose an activity that highly correlates with your most successful users and focus on how you can increase the number and share of users who complete that behavior.

2. A CUSTOMER SATISFACTION METRIC (EX. NPS)

While the impact of a higher Net Promoter Score (NPS) on your business or product may not be immediately visible, the tried and true metric is highly correlated with lower churn. Plus, it's incredibly easy to collect and companies like Delighted and Woobox can help you easily monitor the statistic over time and the reasons behind variations.

Still don't have enough customers to reach any sort of significance with an NPS survey? That's completely fine. Reach out to every 5th or 10th new customer directly yourself after they have used your product. Ask them to rate your product on a 1 – 10 scale at the end of your email/call/Intercom message.

Congratulations, you just started collecting satisfaction data.

3. AN ENGAGEMENT METRIC

For most digital products, engagement is a key sign of success. If your product is incredibly difficult for customers to live without, you've succeeded.

As a new Product Manager, you can either pick a count metric like monthly active users (unique users in a calendar month) or a proportion metric like percent of customers with a second login (i.e. non-abandoners). By tracking engagement rates closely, you'll know if your product is consistently getting better at bringing users back for more.

GETTING QUALITATIVE

We began this chapter by talking about the importance of a strong connection between a Product Manager and all available data surrounding his/her product or his/her new feature. However, our discussion so far largely left out a significant portion of analysis that needs to be completed by the Product Manager: qualitative analysis.

Earlier, we briefly discussed the importance of qualitative analysis through the testing cycle, but we didn't dive into the specifics on how a Product Manager can successfully adopt this essential counterpart to quantitative analysis.

1. SURVEY YOUR USERS AT KEY EVENTS

Did a user just complete a key "activity"? Survey a percentage of these users with a free tool like Hotjar or Qualaroo to see what they thought of the experience and what they would change, add, or remove.

Did a user just cancel their service from your account management page? Make sure you survey them before they can fully complete the cancellation process. Ask them:

- Why would you like to cancel?
- Was there anything we could have done differently?
- Would you like to speak to someone? Sometimes this is all it takes to make a save!

Has a user been inactive for 30 days? Make sure you have an automatic email and survey in place to re-engage these users or at least try to learn about why they stopped using your product.

2. IDENTIFY PROMOTERS DISGUISED AS DETRACTORS

When you get negative responses to you NPS survey (scores from 1-6), dive deep and try to understand what led to their poor perception of your product. Many times, you'll find that your detractors are often promoters in disguise. They liked features 1 and 2, but ran into a bug on feature 3, which destroyed their experience.

Engage these users and you'll quickly build a population of people that aren't afraid to give honest and open feedback on new features, even if it stings a little. Remember that Alpha population we worked on building in Chapter 7? These (hopefully temporary) detractors would be a great addition!

3. HOW DOES A PRODUCT MANAGER SHARE OR PRESENT DATA?

Slow down! We'll talk more about sharing data with the organization and externally in the next two chapters. For now, let's discuss sharing key performance data with your team only.

In Chapter 5, we talked about building the right team. Along with that building process, you should have built a detailed understanding of each of your team members.

Are they excited to stand up against a challenge or do they need a pep-talk each time they try something new?

If they see a disturbing change in trends, do they back-peddle or confront the challenge head-on in an effort to reverse it?

From this place of understanding, a Product Manager should know what type and what depth of data they can share with the team.

Are you a new Product Manager who doesn't know your team well enough yet? No problem, keep it simple, follow the ACE metrics for now. As your team gets comfortable with these key performance indicators, you can expand to more niche analytics.

Consistency and focus are incredibly important for teams of all levels of experience and skill.

4. WHEN IS "GUT FEEL" OK?

Quantitative and Qualitative Analytics are the best friends of a Product Manager building a new product, developing a new feature, or improving an existing product. However, there are many situations when data either isn't available, takes too long to access, or simply isn't valuable.

In these situations, what should a Product Manager do? An effective PM, in an absence-of-data environment, should use their best judgment and incorporate the following factors to make a decision:

1. What does the customer experience look like with the different decision options?
2. What are the risks of this decision?
3. Who does this decision benefit/who does it impact negatively?
4. What are the costs of the different options?

An essential part of making this "data-less" decision is building a foundation for future analytical confirmation or refutation of the "gut feel" decision. By setting up this tracking, the effective PM will ensure that they either validate their decision or pivot quickly from it.

A **Bad Product Manager** relies on his analytics team to pull data on product performance.

A **Good Product Manager** is consistently looking for interesting data to help inform his product development. He/She understands what information is significant and what is just for "vanity".

A **Great Product Manager** has a rabid appetite for data, but also understands its limitations. He/She doesn't rely on others often to pull data, as he/she learns more from the raw data than from someone else's interpretation. He/She is skeptical of other's conclusions and has an insatiable curiosity to understand customer behaviors better. If there isn't tracking, a great Product Manager adds tracking immediately. A great Product Manager is a great analyst.

9. TRANSFORMING YOUR MVP INTO A FULL PRODUCT

PROGRAMMING IS LIKE SEX. ONE MISTAKE AND YOU HAVE TO SUPPORT IT FOR THE REST OF YOUR LIFE

Michael Sinz

You've identified and understood a key problem, sold a solution to management, built your team, released a successful MVP that validated or invalidated several key hypotheses. What's next?

Now it's time to take your MVP to a "full-featured", bona-fide product. Wait, didn't I do this with my beta release? Not quite, although you may have gotten close, depending on what level of finish you chose (MVP/MLP/MRP).

First, in order to decide what should be included in your full-featured product, let's start by evaluating the performance of your MVP.

WHICH FEATURES DID CUSTOMERS LOVE?

How do you know customers loved these features? Look for a wide range of feedback sources, including both qualitative and quantitative data. Also, look for patterns deeper in your data.

Even if one feature looks universally popular, it's likely there are sub-groups who used this feature obsessively and those who were less enthused about it. By segmenting these groups, you're also already helping your marketing organization better understand the target customers.

WHAT FEATURE SET DOES YOUR CURRENT MVP HAVE?

A feature or product can be used in many ways by customers. Some products, while simple, are insanely addictive. They are the first thought many people have in the morning and the last thought they have at night. Think TikTok, Tinder, or Candy Crush here.

Other products, while certainly still successful, only fill a specific purpose in a person's life. For example, products like Salesforce, Microsoft Office, and Adobe Analytics are only valuable for most people while they are at work.

Some features or products just aren't addictive. They serve a purpose at a point in time and aren't incredibly useful after that purpose is accomplished. For example, a cover photo builder for Facebook is a great feature for a Social Media Management product, but how often does a person need to change their cover photo? Would someone really pay for that feature? Maybe, but you'll have to work hard to make it addictive.

WHICH FEATURES DID THEY HATE (OR JUST NOT USE)?

Now that we're a little more educated on major feature categories, what features did your customers HATE in your MVP?

Keep in mind, a feature that isn't used is even worse than a feature that gets negative feedback. A feature that's not used is either completely devoid of value, or you're doing a very poor job of education your users. Regardless, this is a failure.

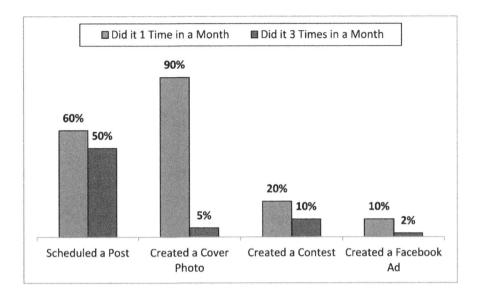

CONDUCT A FEATURE AUDIT

Imagine you just got back the above results from your analytics team on your new Social Media Marketing MVP.

The blue bar is the percent of users that completed the action 1 time in the past month and the red bar is the percent of users that completed the action 3 times in the past month.

WHERE WOULD YOU INVEST (FEATURE WISE) FOR THIS MVP?

The cover photo feature initial usage appears to be incredibly strong. Getting 90% of your users to do anything (even accept free money or free services) is incredibly hard. However, it looks like the depth of this feature is not great; users seem to use this service once and then not again.

Scheduling posts starts much less strongly than cover photos, but interestingly, this feature persists in usage over time. Almost all of the users trying this feature once use it at least three times. This extremely high level of feature retention is also very rare.

At first, it also appears that both Contests and Facebook Ads seem to provide some value to users. However, each captures a pretty small portion of usage from our customers.

If I was presented with this feature audit from an MVP release, I would immediately shut down the contests and ads features. Next, I would figure out how to sequence the cover photo and post scheduling features together to capture the incredible initial usage of the cover photo feature and the strong retention of the post scheduling feature.

BUT WAIT, WHY NOT KEEP THE FEATURES YOU HAVE BUILT ALREADY?

Features, even the ones you've built already, have *costs* to maintain. More features are not always better; in fact, they're almost always worse. Why?

First, these features strain your support team. Take a quick minute and think up all of the ways the contests and ads features could break. In the time it took you to read that sentence, I already have 5 different failure points for these two features.

Next, these low-usage features are a distraction to your team. If your vision is to build the best post scheduling product, your team will naturally wonder: "Why then do we have this contests feature?" Additionally, extra non-core features can negatively impact the feature you care about. If you redesign your navigation UI, you'll still have to include that secondary or tertiary feature, when there could likely be a better design focused around the core, popular feature only.

Finally, would you rather build basic enhancements for features that only 20% of users use or significant enhancements for a feature used by 75% of your users?

Remember that saying no is the most important job of the Product Manager. After interpreting your MVP results, you have a huge opportunity to say no, keep your team focused, and place your product on a successful strategic path.

Chances are, even with a successful MVP like the one described earlier, you'll end up with more questions than answers on the future of your product. For that reason, you should treat your full product release as another great opportunity to validate a new, more significant, set of hypotheses.

If you validated that customers would sign up for the product and use it once with your MVP, now try to validate that they will pay for certain parts of the product. If you determined that scheduling was the key feature in your MVP release as we saw in the data above, try to make that feature even deeper and stickier with your post-MVP product.

While an MVP is often the time when the most learning occurs in product development, the post-MVP hypothesis validation is just as important for the long-term success of the product and your company.

WHAT DOES SOFTWARE DEVELOPMENT IN POST-MVP LOOK LIKE?

After you've decided on the feature set you want to pursue for your post-MVP product, what does development actually look like? How is it this period different than the pre-MVP world where we moved fast and broke things?

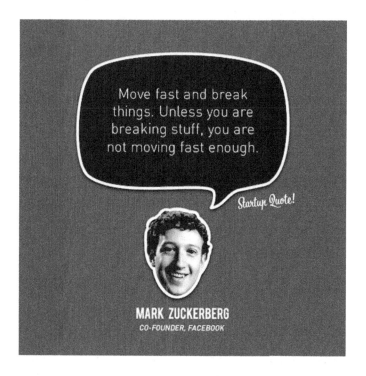

Again, your focus will depend on the size of your company, but a post-MVP product certainly needs more stability. Save yourself many, many, many future headaches by setting up plenty of upfront monitoring. DataDog and Pingdom are two personal favorites.

Additionally, from a technology perspective, you'll want to simplify your product wherever you can to avoid maintenance problems in the future.

Have your development leads search for hastily written MVP code to "refactor". Yes, refactoring may be one of the most frustrating words for a Product Manager to hear as it doesn't tie directly to user-facing output, this is the time to do it. Haven't heard of refactoring?

Check out the Agile Urban Dictionary at the end of this book for the real definition.

WHAT SHOULD I BE THINKING ABOUT AS THE TEAM IS WORKING?

As the team enters the post-MVP build cycle, it's time to start thinking about marketing. As we'll see in the coming chapter, the Product Manager as a CEO is responsible for the success of their product in all functions. This implies that the PM is also essential in the promotion of the full product release.

Post-MVP development isn't about new features and functionality. In addition to stability, you'll likely need to build landing pages, onboarding experiences, upsells, referral programs, and establish your SEO strategy. At this point in the development cycle, you'll find yourself spending as much time with your head of marketing as you do with your engineering team.

This leads to a disturbing trend in product development: As a product gets more mature, the Product Manager spends a smaller and smaller time on actual product development. Much more time is spent on marketing, bug fixes, and incremental feature improvements.

A successful Product Manager finds a way to fight this trend and find opportunities for continued product development.

While it's likely your team will be less excited about this work than the MVP build out, it's your role to motivate them and show them the importance of tackling these challenges.

What they've built so far is great, but it's not sustainable, it's not fully releasable, it's not fully marketable. This upcoming work will take the product and the team to a place where they aren't waking up in the middle of the night worried about the product.

WHAT IS ONBOARDING AND WHY IS IT IMPORTANT?

Onboarding has been a complete game changer with the digital products I've been a part of. Unless you've built a highly intuitive product (and likely, even if you have), onboarding offers an incredible opportunity to collect information about your new customer, personalize their experience, and make them feel successful within minutes of product discovery.

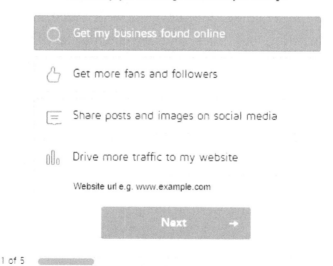

Welcome, Alex's Antiques

Help us customize your social media marketing experience by answering a few quick questions...

PLEASE CHOOSE YOUR PRIMARY GOAL
Don't worry, you can change this later in your settings.

Get my business found online

Get more fans and followers

Share posts and images on social media

Drive more traffic to my website

Website url e.g. www.example.com

Next →

1 of 5   skip

Depending on your specific business, successful user onboarding can lead to step function increases in usage, decreases in churn, and increases in conversion rate.

START BY FOLLOWING "FIVE COMMANDMENTS OF ONBOARDING"

1. Set a goal for your user's behavior
2. Remind users how much better things will be with your product
3. Show the "Emerald City"
4. Use social proof
5. Land a user softly in your product

If you're already hooked, you can learn much more about onboarding here: www.useronboard.com

Samuel Hulick has put together some fantastic insights about what makes onboarding great and also what makes onboarding fail. Plus, he updates his site every couple of weeks with new onboarding teardowns. One of my personal favorites is his Ashley Madison onboarding teardown.

HOW MOTIVATE MY TEAM POST-MVP?

Studies indicate that morale for a software development team is often the lowest in the post-MVP, pre-full product launch time period.

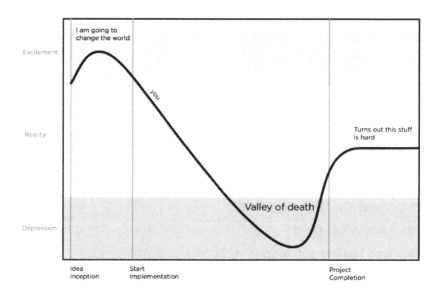

As a Product Manager, you have the responsibility of keeping your team motivated through this difficult period. With the fast-paced and low-oversight MVP-build behind you, here are a few easy things you can do to continue to inspire and motivate your team:

1. Bring some happy customers from the MVP (Alpha or Beta release) into the office and ask them to informally share their experiences with your team over lunch.

2. Read detractor responses from MVP product surveys (insta-bility, missing features, etc.). Ideally choose quotes referenc-ing problems that you've prioritized to be fixed with the full product.

3. Show a comparison of the number of customers currently us-ing the product with a rough projection of those expected to use the product after its full release (should be a dramatic in-crease). I've often found that user growth comparisons are especially successful with motivating my team.

4. Team lunches and events. This should be a part of every step of your development cycle and simply part of being close with your team, but make sure not to skip these just because you're busy or working to a tight deadline. Even though you'll be out of the office for several hours (or even a full day), the break from the average and the bonding across the team is well worth it!

HOW DO I KNOW I'VE REACHED A READY-TO-RELEASE PRODUCT?

Things you'll find yourself saying:

- I'm not quite sure what the next feature we should build is
- We didn't hear any customers mention *that* in our testing
- Are you sure we need translations for Norwegian?

WHAT ARE SOME SIGNS THAT YOU DEFINITELY AREN'T READY TO RE-LEASE?

Things you'll find yourself saying:

- It doesn't work great on Safari *sometimes*
- We aren't sure why it crashes, but it doesn't happen too often
- But no one uses that feature anyway, so not many people will notice
- We'll add analytics after the release as a quick-follow

Releasing to everyone is scary. The stakes are much higher than your Alpha and Beta MVP releases, financials actually matter, and the decisions of you and your team are now exposed to the world. However, if you approach your full release as an opportunity to focus your product, test new hypotheses, and increase stability, you will be in great shape.

A **Bad Product Manager** simply increases the exposure of his/her Beta release and thinks this is adequate for a full release.

A **Good Product Manager** evaluates the performance of their MVP, focuses on the features that matter, and determines what needs to be built before the product can be released to everyone.

A **Great Product Manager** obsesses over MVP performance. They find trends and behaviors hidden within the data and quickly determine what features are worth focusing on and which don't matter. They focus their team and motivate them through this final stage of development in creative ways. Finally, they're focused in this development stage on how their product can be marketed effectively.

10. PROMOTING YOUR PRODUCT RELEASE AND PRODUCT MANAGER AS CEO

There is a significant amount of debate in the Product Manager community about whether a Product Manager should be considered the "CEO" of the product. Individuals who oppose this categorization cite the Product Manager's lack of hiring/firing ability and the general distribution of authority across the team as proof that the PM is not like a CEO at all.

However, despite these differences, a great Product Manager will view him or herself as a CEO, and as responsible for the ultimate success of their product. Even if a piece of the product falls well outside of the Product Manager's comfort zone or traditional responsibilities, the great Product Manager won't ever fully take their hands off the decision making process.

To make this idea more concrete, marketing is one responsibility that traditionally falls outside of the responsibilities of the prototypical Product Manager. But, the great Product Manager still has a strong role to play in this part of the product release. The Product Manager and their team understand the product better than anyone. They know the product's strengths (from both a development and user-focused perspective) and they certainly know its shortcomings.

Finally, a Product Manager often brings a creative perspective and ideas that life-long marketers can't conceive simply because they didn't bring this product to life from nothing.

TRY SOMETHING NEW (EVERY SINGLE TIME)

One of my favorite rules for Product Manager is that **every single launch should include at least 1 tactic you or your company has never tried before.** This could be as simple or traditional as a launch party for the release or as sophisticated as a guerilla marketing cam-

93

paign within your targeted user population. Get creative, have fun, and do something new **every single time**.

Although I strongly believe the Product Manager should be the CEO of the product, it's definitely ok to let marketing develop the plan for a product release, but you should be heavily involved in shaping that initial plan to one that you think will be most successful for the product.

Marketing is almost always working off of their **assumptions** about who the customer will be and the perceived capabilities of the product. As the Product Manager, you know significantly more about the use-cases, strengths, and weaknesses of the product you've built or improved. You know what features and experiences should be emphasized again and again and what parts of your application should be avoided. You know when to make comparisons to competitors and when not to.

A Product Manager should also be a content producer and an evangelist for both their product and the general field that their product operates in. First, start as an internal promoter. Internal promotion includes hosting events like lunch and learns, demos, and expert speakers. This promotion helps educate and excite your colleagues about what you're building and why you're building it.

Blog posts are also a Product Manager best friend. They are an opportunity to establish a position of credibility and subject matter expertise before product release and promotion. They also offer an opportunity to show a little bit of what is "behind the curtain" of development and why certain product decisions were made to you most avid users and influencers. In the past five years at Vistaprint, Upside Travel, and ICX Media, I've written over 75 blog posts on a wide variety of topics. If you haven't had enough of me and my writing yet, you can find many of those posts here: Alex Mitchell's Blog Posts

Another great content medium to support your product marketing is analytical research. This category can also include whitepapers and long-form content. The idea here is that you're already doing a large amount of research and analytics for your product, so why not share what you've learned? You'll want to make sure not to share too much, but there's very low risk that sharing information about your product will benefit competitors. For a company that shares absolutely everything and has built a great brand from it, check out Buffer and their blog.

Finally, a great Product Manager can help support their products and their company's brand by being a frequent attendee and participant at conferences. New to Product Management? Find a niche of product that you're incredibly interested in and start developing your expertise.

Learn from the experts, try new things, and build your own theories. Before long, you'll have enough experience to apply for speaking opportunities at product conferences. Once there, you have a great opportunity to share your beliefs as well as how your company and your product support those ideas. Double points for you and your product.

Saying the Product Manager is the CEO of the product is controversial, but it's true. The Product Manager should know the most about the product, have the highest investment in its success, and is primarily responsible for motivating their team to achieve more. This definitely doesn't mean a Product Manager should operate in isolation. Rather, they should engage their marketing team, their support team, and other Product Managers at appropriate times to help give their product the highest likelihood of success.

A **Bad Product Manager** hands off their product to the "marketing team" and doesn't participate in the product promotion process.

A **Good Product Manager** starts thinking about marketing early in the build process, incorporating the brainstorming he/she and others completed on the user problem into a solution that not only can be delivered to customers, but also explained and understood.

A **Great Product Manager** owns the marketing of their product. This does not mean they do all of the work to market their new product or feature, but rather, means that they are involved with all major marketing decisions, share the voice of the customer (or potential customer), and makes sure their product UX aligns with the target audience. A Great Product Manager also markets every product differently, incorporating his/her knowledge of product quality, customer expertise, and product roadmap into account.

11. DEFINING AND SHARING SUCCESS

We talked in previous chapters about the importance of tracking quantitative and qualitative analytics throughout the development process and establishing you're A-C-E metrics. However, I want to talk about the importance of setting and communicating goals effectively both within and outside of your team. Sound easy enough? Trust me, it's not.

WHAT TYPE OF LONG-TERM GOALS SHOULD I SET?

Some goals you choose to set yourself, others are assigned or mandated to you. The importance of these goals varies widely by the stage of the development cycle.

Internal Team Goals

Internal team goals should be your most aggressive and also are often your least informed. It's ok to make these goals BIG or a little more difficult to track. These goals are just as much about vision as they are about tracking. The main part to focus on here is "internal".

Don't lose the trust of your team by sharing aggressive internal goals externally. Besides losing their confidence, you'll also quickly realize that many of these goals are way off! Internal team goals are your "rough draft" of project goals.

Again, I'd encourage you to check out John Doerr's Measure What Matters to learn more about setting aggressive and trackable goals in the form of Objectives and Key Results (OKRs):

Still confused? Here are some internal team goals we set at Pagemodo for our iOS app:

1. Rank #1 for Social Media Marketing Apps in the Apple App Store by January 1, 20xx
2. Achieve 20% desktop subscriber penetration by February 15, 20xx
3. Reach 50% 1 week retention of App users by March 15, 20xx

These goals are **aggressive and time-bound**. However, they continue to help focus our team on key goals around usage, retention, and promotion. Shared externally, these type of goals could hurt your team or lead to unrealistic expectations from external stakeholders. However, shared internally, these goals will fire up your team and get them excited about the future.

ACE Goals with Leadership Team

In Chapter 8, we reviewed A-C-E goals and how they can be a catalyst for strong product development. These are safe goals to communicate with your leadership team. How aggressive should you be with these goals? There's no easy answer.

Think again about the character of you company. Similar to the way you determined what problem to solve, how to solve it, and how you defined your MVP, you'll want to apply the same level of rigor to setting your ACE goals.

Before establishing your targets with your leadership team, map your upcoming product development to ACE. Which initiatives do you think will impact Activity, which will impact Churn, which will impact Engagement?

Once you've mapped out key near-term development initiatives to these goals, start estimating roughly what type of impact you think they will have. It's ok to stay general here: High, Medium, Low impact will do.

From this exercise, you should be able to get a feel for which metrics have the opportunity to move significantly and which are going to be very challenging to impact in the short-term. Draft your goals accordingly and realistically.

Don't sandbag (setting incredibly easy to attain goals); however, exceeding goals here is your best opportunity for building your brand as a successful Product Manager.

Also, make sure to over-communicate short-term. This is agile development, not fixed development. Don't be forced into locking goals for an entire fiscal year. In that time period, budgets change, teams change, the environment changes, and opportunities change. The ideal time to plan and revisit goals is quarterly.

This will provide enough foresight to be valuable to leadership and other stakeholders while giving you enough control as a Product Manager to account for a shifting climate.

Financial Goals

For immature products, committing to financial goals can be very dangerous. Assessing demand and price sensitivity of a nascent industry is very challenging and usually very inaccurate. It's for this reason that I strongly discourage committing to direct financial goals, meaning bookings and revenue, in the early stages of a product's life, before demand has been validated.

For mature products that you're developing additional features for, financial goals can be more beneficial and significantly more accurate. For example, if you're designing a new feature, you should be able to realistically model what % of existing users will upgrade to use the new feature, projected churn impacts, and additional costs incurred.

However, make sure that your commitments to financial goals don't discourage vital product development. Meaning, don't let financial goal pressure force you into price increases or marketing tricks. Make sure you buy yourself and your team enough space to allow for core product development. For financial goals, keep the time horizon short as well. Again, things change incredibly quickly and you want to make sure you don't lock in goals that quickly become unrealistic in 3 months.

SHARING GOAL PERFORMANCE

There is a lot going on in your organization. There is a lot going on in every organization. Regardless of the structure of your company, human nature tells us that people are primarily self-interested. It's difficult to break through that fact with your product and your message, but here are the secrets how.

1. SHARE BIG

As we discussed earlier, avoid Vanity Metrics, but share the biggest metrics you can. By big, I mean the metrics that have the biggest potential to impact your overall business. Make it impossible for listeners to avoid understanding that your team can and will change the entire business.

2. SHARE SIMPLE

While you may understand cohort based trending, matched-pairs comparisons, and multi-level segmentation, your diverse audience certainly does not. While you Share BIG, also make sure you Share SIMPLE. Your metrics need to be tangible and they can almost always be shared in a few simple words or numbers.

3. SHARE MEMORABLE

If you've shared BIG and shared SIMPLE, you're well on your way to sharing MEMORABLE, but just because you're getting close, doesn't mean you're there quite yet. Your metrics should be internally viral. They should be fun to say and repeat. In a company-wide or team-wide meeting, many people share information; you want yours to be remembered.

Research suggests that the best way to help your audience remember what you say is to tell a story. For example, if your BIG/SIMPLE metric is that you **increased publish/key activity rate by 15% in the last quarter**, tell a story about a few of the customers who especially benefitted from the changes you made.

Remember that your team always comes first for sharing success; recognition should never be accepted by the Product Manager. The Product Manager is a deep diving analyst who shares interesting trends, captivating stories, and a continued vision for the product.

A **Bad Product Manager** doesn't set goals, so they can't fail. When he/she rarely succeeds, they take the credit.

A **Good Product Manager** sets aggressive goals and shares them with their team on a frequent basis to keep them focused. They understand the difference between short, mid, and long-term goals and know the right places to share and refer to each. When they share data, they do a pretty good job, but they don't stand out.

A **Great Product Manager** sets the right goals at the right time to motivate their team and the entire organization. These goals cover all major parts of the development cycle and help the team focus and make decisions without constant reinforcement from the Product Manager. When a great Product Manager shares data with the organization, everyone remembers the key points and everyone is motivated to achieve more. They always direct the credit to their team.

12. SUPPORTING YOUR PRODUCT

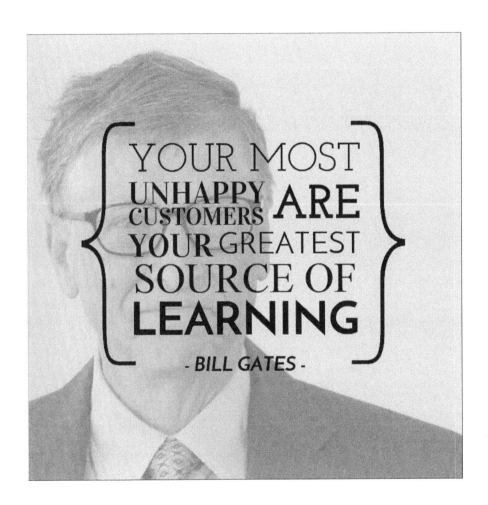

After you launch a product, you own it forever.

While that may be a little bit of an exaggeration; you do own your products beyond your current role, beyond your current team, and even beyond your current company. That product is not only now part of your portfolio, its part of you.

The positive aspects of your product will support your future goals and help you achieve success, while the negative parts will relentlessly cling to you like that "friend" from high school that you just can't get rid of.

This ownership doesn't simply extend to the occasional question you get from leadership or that new Product Manager on why something was done a certain way or where to find a certain piece of documentation. Your ownership extends to the relationship you have with your support team, it extends to the new set of engineers who have to maintain the product, and it extends to your perception as a quality Product Manager.

DON'T BECOME AN ENEMY OF YOUR SUPPORT TEAM

While we've definitely encouraged understanding your effort /return trade off many times in this book, remember this: If you build a crappy product that needs constant maintenance and customer support, even one that has a positive ROI for the business, you'll make enemies across your company.

In this case, your engineers and support agents will often speak louder than your customers and provide a constant reminder of just how unstable things are. I would much rather build small, focused, stable applications than large, crappy ones that need constant patches.

Your support department should be a vital component of your mature, post-release product. They should own your **Net Promoter Score** and be willing and able to identify risks to long term stability from both a user and development perspective.

Are bugs and performance getting to critical levels?

What do customers request most?

Note: This doesn't mean we need to build these features.

What do they complain about most?

What admin features can make support's job significantly easier?

It's your job as a Product Manager to interpret these often un-focused narratives of the customer experience and determine which bugs, performance issues, and support tools are worth fixing or building.

A **Bad Product Manager** assumes that once a product has been launched, his/her job is done.

A **Good Product Manager** has a strong relationship with their support team because they know it's the front-line of customer feedback.

A **Great Product Manager** listens closely to their support group. More importantly, they know how to rank customer issues by total impact (number of customers impacted), strategic priority, risk to other parts of the product/company, and ease of resolution. They know if something needs to be fixed now, fixed later, or fixed never, and they always are honest with their colleagues.

13. INTEGRATING YOUR PRODUCT

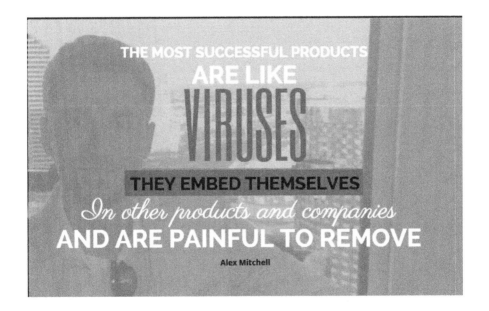

Although I probably scared you in the last chapter by saying you own the products you build forever, this is actually a positive outcome of product development. Long-lived products may be scary from a development and maintenance perspective, but they are incredibly exciting from a financial and long-term business impact perspective.

As a Product Manager, you should integrate your product into other products and services that your company offers. For example, if you're building a service that helps small businesses get listed in online directories (YP.com, Yahoo, Yelp), your opportunities for integrations are almost limitless.

If a user is listed on Yelp, you can pull in Yelp reviews with the Yelp API and offer recommendations on how to respond to existing Yelp reviews and solicit new ones.

You could integrate your product with a website builder (Webs, Weebly, Wix, Squarespace) to offer pre-populated websites to users of this product, built from the wealth of knowledge you already have about their business.

Finally, you could even integrate easy-to-use advertising solutions for Google and Facebook to help these small business customers get even more value out of their newly created online presences.

While some standalone products can live on very long period of time without integrations, these are certainly the exception and not the rule.

Try to name more than 5 products that lasted 5 years without any integrations with other services. It isn't easy. Internal and external integrations are vital to the long term success and viability of your product.

However, make sure to avoid a few common issues with integrations of both internal and external product integrations. You should make sure any cross-sell offers you extend are carefully considered:

- What percent of people who see this offer is it relevant for?
- Conversely, what percent of people see this message and think we've lost our mind?
- How frictionless is the offer process for customers who accept? Is there a single login?
- Is information shared between products?
- Can I see all of the products I own in one place?

Similar to other development, many of the concepts of MVP extend strongly to integrations and cross-sells. It's incredibly easy to "vapor test" integrations and offers or assess approximate demand through customer surveys. Don't commit your developer's time to an extensive build out of cross-sell offers and integrations without some decent analytical proof.

With integrations, the product development cycle comes full circle back to ideation:

- Where are the biggest opportunities to introduce a user to complementary products?
- Can we vapor test product offers to find conversion rate before connecting them fully?
- How do different channels (email, in-app, social, targeted ads) respond differently to cross-sell offers?
- How do different customer segments and use-cases respond to offers?

Once you've tested offers and integrations, commit to tackling the top ones with your team. Make sure to stress how this work will help your product survive longer and reach more people.

A **Bad Product Manager** builds products in isolation. They don't care about how their products or features fit into the larger goals of the organization.

A **Good Product Manager** thinks about how users move between products (i.e. the customer lifecycle) and tries to insert their product at the right stage with appropriate messaging.

A **Great Product Manager** embeds their product within other internal and external products at appropriate contextual moments. They think from a user-focused perspective (i.e. "Would my product benefit a user of another product at this key point?"). A great Product Manager also leverages data from other products wherever possible in his own product. Does one of your products have page view and analytics tracking? Can you leverage that information as a powerful cross-sell from inside the product you're currently building?

CONCLUSION

It was an absolutely incredible experience writing this book. Updating it for the 2nd edition with many new things I've learned over the past 4 years has been just as fun!

I would like to sincerely thank my fellow Product Managers, colleagues, friends, and family for helping me refine my disparate thoughts, arguments, and insights, making them significantly more coherent and more enjoyable to read.

It is my sincere hope that regardless of your experience level as a Product Manager, this book has helped you envision the Product Manager you want to become. I also hope that this handbook has given you plenty of ideas for how you can get there.

I look forward to your feedback (both positive and negative welcomed) and thank you for reading!

Alex Mitchell

You can also find me at:

www.alexmitchell.co
www.twitter.com/amitch5903
www.medium.com/@amitch5903
www.linkedin.com/alexmitchell15
www.angel.co/amitch5903

*P.S. Don't forget about all of the **bonus material***
in the appendix sections!

A1. URBAN DICTIONARY FOR PRODUCT MANAGERS

Sources

http://agiledictionary.com

http://www.solutionsiq.com/agile-glossary/kanban

BACKLOG

Traditional Definition: An ever-evolving list of product requirements, prioritized by the customer (or customer representative), that conveys to an Agile team which features to implement first.

Real Definition: The ever-changing bible of the Product Manager. Every idea, however far-fetched, should be contained in the backlog of the Product Manager.

As you move higher and higher in the backlog, the descriptions should increase in length, potential KPIs of interest should be listed, wireframes should be included, and the overall level of thought put into the user story should increase.

While a story near the bottom of the backlog may be nothing but a title, a story near the top of the backlog likely contains all the details that a developer would need to start coding today.

EPIC

Traditional Definition: A very large user story that is eventually broken down into smaller stories. Epics are often used as placeholders for new ideas that have not been thought out fully or whose full elaboration has been deferred until actually needed.

Real Definition: A "theme" that groups a series of tickets. This theme could be something like "External Site Redesign" or "Add Pinterest to Posting Destinations". This theme is clear and contains all of the tickets to achieve that goal.

The great thing about an epic is it offers the Product Manager a great opportunity to share a vision. On a strong team, developers, designers, and testers will highlight user stories missing from epics because the vision is that crisp. Epics should be designed so well that even in the absence of individual stories, the team could determine the work needed.

ESTIMATION

Traditional Definition: The process of agreeing on a size measurement for the stories or tasks in a product backlog. On agile projects, estimation is done by the team responsible for delivering the work, usually using a planning game.

Real Definition: The meeting that brings the backlog to life. A non-estimated story may as well be dead to the Product Manager and to the team. Once user stories are estimated, the Product Manager has a rough idea of the work needed to bring it to life. Additionally, the estimation meeting is an opportunity to educate the Product Manager on the cost of several different potential paths to deliver the feature to users.

GROOMING

Traditional Definition: During this meeting, everyone helps prepare the backlog for the sprint planning meeting. This usually includes adding new stories and epics, extracting stories from existing epics, and estimating effort for existing stories.

Real Definition: The place to add the details to the skeleton tickets created by the Product Manager. I've found it most successful to rotate team members through this meeting and have ½ attend each week. Too many team members and you'll get slowed down by pursuing too many different technical solutions. Too few and you'll miss possible resolutions to the user story.

IMPEDIMENT

Traditional Definition: Any obstacle preventing a developer or team from completing work.

Real Definition: A problem that the team encounters and the Product Manager is responsible for finding the resources to solve. A key purpose of the Product Manager is the make the lives of their developers easier.

KANBAN

Traditional Definition: Kanban visually represents the state of work in process. Unlike a task board, the Kanban constrains how much work in process is permitted to occur at the same time. The purpose of limiting work in process is to reduce bottlenecks and increase throughput by optimizing that segment of the value stream that is the subject of the Kanban.

Real Definition: A short term solution to the "I have no clue how much work this team can do, how hard the work is, or how long it will take" problem. Let's just get as much shit done as quickly as we can. In my opinion, every Kanban team should strive to grow into sprint planning as soon as possible.

MINIMUM VIABLE PRODUCT (MVP)

Traditional Definition: The smallest thing we can test to enable one cycle of the build – measure – learn loop. As opposed to Minimum

Marketable Feature (MMF) that is the smallest thing that delivers a user value.

Real Definition: When we can finally say – "Ship it!"

REFACTORING

Traditional Definition: Changing existing software code in order to improve the overall design. Refactoring normally doesn't change the observable behavior of the software; it improves its internal structure.

Real Definition: **ARRRRGGGGHHH**, but necessary to make sure your product doesn't implode.

RETROSPECTIVE

Traditional Definition: An Agile retrospective is a meeting that's held at the end of iteration in Agile software development (ASD). During the retrospective, the team reflects on what happened in the iteration and identifies actions for improvement going forward.

Real Definition: A therapy session for the team. An opportunity to vent + reflect about bad decisions that were made. Also, a place to be overly optimistic that everything will change in the next two weeks.

SPIKE

Traditional Definition: A story or task aimed at answering a question or gathering information, rather than producing a shippable product.

Real Definition: A low-cost "early read" on the difficulty of a complex or unfamiliar user story or epic.

SPRINT PLANNING

Traditional Definition: Each sprint begins with a sprint planning meeting, the activity that prioritizes and identifies stories and concrete tasks for the next sprint.

Real Definition: A meeting where the Product Manager brings the priorities and the team commits to how much they think they can conservatively complete in the sprint. Commitment strategies vary by team.

STANDUP

Traditional Definition: A daily team meeting held to provide a status update to the team members. The 'semi-real-time' status allows participants to know about potential challenges as well as coordinate efforts to resolve difficult and/or time-consuming issues.

Real Definition: A rapid-fire development team recap (15 minutes) of yesterday and plan for today. Your best chance as a Product Manager to keep the team focused, spot problems before they get big, and help with anything that could distract the team.

STORY

Traditional Definition: An Agile requirement, stated as a sentence or two of plain English. A user story is often expressed from the user's point of view, and describes a unit of desired functionality.

Real Definition: A brief description of the value we're going to deliver to our customers.

VELOCITY

Traditional Definition: The rate at which a team completes work, used not to measure progress per se, but to accurately estimate the team's capacity for future iterations and guide the team and Product Manager in planning upcoming iterations.

Real Definition: The answer to: "How much can this team get done in 2 weeks?" However, don't track velocity as a KPI – it can widely vary with the stage of the project, the learning curve for new development languages, team departures/additions, and other factors.

WATERFALL

Traditional Definition: The traditional method for developing and delivering software. The Waterfall method breaks a project into discrete stages. In a Waterfall process, each step must be completed before moving on to the next, and all steps in the process must be completed before any value is delivered to the customer.

Real Definition: People really used to develop like this!? AKA: The way the government still works.

A2. DEVELOPMENT CHECKLISTS TO KEEP YOU SANE

IDENTIFYING, UNDERSTANDING, AND IDEATING ON A PROBLEM

☑	Create a list of features that your current products are missing.
☑	List the worst bugs (in terms of total impact to your business) in your current products and how much you think they cost you.
☑	Group your products into 3 categories: Market Leaders, Average Performers, and Underperformers. Discuss why each product is in its respective column.
☑	Give each member of your team a list of missing features, horrific bugs, and key customer problems that your company doesn't address today. Have them rank which they would be **most excited about solving.**
☑	Interview current customers who are experiencing issues or lack of functionality with your products. Share results with your team. Better yet, have them be a part of the interviews.

EXPLORING SOLUTIONS TO A PROBLEM

☑	What are the top 3 **core competencies** of your company? Be honest.
☑	What are the top 3 **major weaknesses** of your company? Be even more honest.
☑	What are some new areas of product opportunity for your

	company **related** to your current business?
☑	What are some new areas of product opportunity for your company **unrelated** to your current business?
☑	For each opportunity, write down an **ideal solution**, a **practical solution**, and a **crappy but functional** solution. How long does each take? What do the components of each solution look like?
☑	Is anyone else solving this problem today? Rate how well each problem you've identified is being solved today.
☑	List potential ways you can test each potential solution to a customer problem.

SELLING YOUR SOLUTION

☑	Identify all of your key stakeholders. Include their position, their level of decision rights (low, medium, high), and their motivations.
☑	List all of the potential negative responses to your proposed solution(s).
☑	List all of your rebuttals to those negative responses.
☑	Identify all of the people that you can share your solution with that are not on your team or in the key stakeholders list. Get feedback from them before you start pitching.
☑	Secure any and all data relevant to supporting your solution.

☑	Set a time period for your key hypothesis validation or refutation. When will you know whether to continue forward or to end the project?
☑	What **3 key metrics (A-C-E)** will tell you whether you are successful or not? By what date do you want to improve them by what amount?

BUILDING YOUR TEAM

☑	List key attributes of the ideal team for building a solution to the key customer problem. What couldn't you live without?
☑	Identify several team-size scenarios (famine, average, and feast) and how each scenario would impact your time to completion. Include the specific positions you would need in each case (ex. QA, Design, UX, Front-end DEV, Back-end DEV, Senior DEV).
☑	Determine the top 5 key skills that someone in each of the above roles should have.
☑	Rank your current team members across these key skills. Where are you exceptional, where are you deficient? This can be fun! Make trading cards for each team member to make it more interactive.
☑	Plan a week of team-building exercises. Set your norms, sell (and get your team to buy) a vision, determine goals and the key hypotheses you hope to test.

BUILDING YOUR MVP

☑	What is your key hypothesis or hypotheses?
☑	What metrics will validate or invalidate this hypothesis? (A-C-E). When will you be able to validate/invalidate by?
☑	List all the parts of the project that could be purchased instead of built. Refer to the Build vs. Buy chapter to decide how to handle each.
☑	How will you prototype?
☑	Who will you release to first outside of the team?
☑	What does your Alpha release look like? Where does your Alpha population come from?
☑	How will you know you can move beyond Alpha?
☑	What does your Beta release look like?
☑	How will you know you can move beyond Beta?
☑	List all the people you'll rely in (both inside and outside of your team) to bring your MVP to users.
☑	What is a reasonable time to test your hypothesis?
☑	How much time do you think you have with your stakeholders to prove value?

PROMOTING YOUR PRODUCT RELEASE

☑	List out all the channels of your Launch strategy. Include the size of the opportunity (Small/Medium/Large), the cost of the channel, and your expectations.
☑	Write down all the stakeholders in your launch. This list should include everyone who is helping in marketing, product, support, and other groups.
☑	What is (at least) one brand-new thing are you doing with this release?
☑	Write at least one blog post to promote your upcoming product release.
☑	Write a long-form piece of content, either analytical or reflection, that can be released after your product launch.

SUPPORTING YOUR PRODUCT AND INTEGRATION

☑	Meet with your support group to discuss feedback from customers and high value issues with the product. Empower them to suggest high priority fixes to you and your team.
☑	Share your NPS data with your support team and have them "own" this metric.
☑	Consider building simple tools for support or integrating support services (Intercom/Olark) to further strengthen the bond between your team, you, and your support group.

☑	Do a one day hackathon for your support organization.
☑	Integrate your product with at least one other product that your company offers.
☑	Integrate your product with at least one external company or product.
☑	Consider how your product fits into the lifecycle of a customer of your company. How can other products your company offers integrate your product or cross-sell your product?

A3. 100 PRODUCTS FOR THE PRODUCT MANAGER

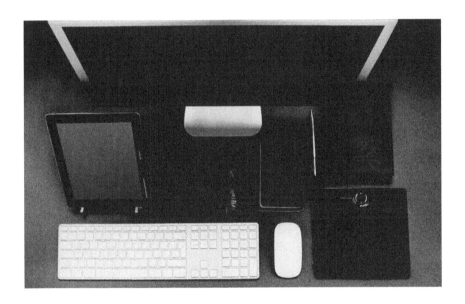

IDEA MANAGEMENT AND SYNDICATION

- **Medium:** Everyone's stories and ideas.
- **Javelin:** Test your startup idea without wasting time or money.
- **Germ.io:** Get from idea to execution.
- **Skitch by Evernote:** Your ideas become reality faster.

SURVEYS AND A/B TESTING

- **Typeform:** Free beautiful online survey & form builder.
- **Qualaroo:** Get feedback from users with an interactive survey widget.
- **Optimizely:** One optimization platform for websites and mobile apps.

LEARN

- **Coursera:** Free online classes from 80+ top universities & organizations.
- **Khan Academy:** Free, world-class education for anyone, anywhere.
- **Skillshare:** Unlock your creativity with free online classes & projects.
- **Codecademy:** Learn to code interactively, for free.
- How to Start a Startup: **As an Audio Podcast** or **As Online Course**
- **Startup Notes:** Startup School invites amazing founders to tell their story.
- **ThePitch (Podcast):** Where founders pitch their startups to investors.

- **Pricing Course:** A free 9 day course on charging what you're worth.
- **GrowthHackers:** Exactly what it sounds like.

EMAIL MANAGEMENT

- **Mailchimp:** Send 12,000 emails to 2,000 subscribers for free.
- **ManyContactsBar:** Free contact form sits on top of your website.
- **Hello Bar:** Get more email subscribers.
- **Sumome List Builder:** Collect email addresses with light box popover.
- **Sumome Scroll Box:** Capture more email addresses, politely.

ORGANIZE & COLLABORATE

- **Trello:** Keeps track of everything.
- **Evernote:** The workspace for your life's work.
- **Dropbox:** Free space up to 2GB.
- **Slack:** Free for unlimited users with few limited features.
- **Google Hangouts:** Bring conversations to life with photos, emoji and group video calls.
- **Join.me:** Free screen sharing and video/phone calls.
- **FreeConferenceCall:** Decent conference call quality (even international) for $0.

SUPPORT AND ENGAGE YOUR CUSTOMERS

- **Intercom:** A fundamentally new way to communicate with your customers.
- **Zendesk:** Brings companies and their customers closer together.

MOBILE

- **Mobile Action:** Killer app store optimization and analytics platform. All you need in addition to iTunes tracking to understand your app under <100k downloads.
- **Parse:** A free push notification service (up to 1MM messages/month) to integrate into your app.
- **Apptentive:** The tools you need to listen to, engage with, and retain your mobile customers in-app.

ANALYTICS AND EVENT TRACKING

- **Mixpanel:** Define and track events, segments, and funnels quickly and easily.
- **Heap:** Mixpanel without any development work needed to create events.
- **Google Analytics:** Your go-to free platform for tracking site visitors, mapping behaviors, and creating live dashboards.

FIND CONTENT AND TRACK TRENDS

- **Buzzsumo:** Analyze what content performs best for any topic or competitor.
- **Feedly:** Compiles news feeds from a variety of online sources for the user to customize & share.
- **Google Trends:** A new way of displaying trending searches.

SEO + WEBSITE ANALYZERS

- **SimilarWeb:** Analyze website statistics for any domain.
- **Open Site Explorer by Moz:** A comprehensive tool for link analysis.
- **Ahrefs:** Site explorer & backlink checker.

- **Quick Sprout:** Complete analysis of your website.
- **SEO Site Checkup:** SCheck your website's SEO problems for free.
- **SERPs Rank Checker:** Free keyword rank & SERP checker.
- **Google Pagespeed Insights:** Check the performance of your site.
- **Pingdom:** Test the load time of a site.

SCREENSHOTS/MOCKUPS OF APPS AND WEBSITES

- **Dunnnk:** Beautiful mockups.

IMAGE EDITORS

- **Canva:** Amazingly simple graphic design for bloggers.
- **Social Image Resizer Tool:** Create optimized images for social media.

SOCIAL MEDIA + COMMUNITY MANAGEMENT

- **Pagemodo:** Everything you need for a powerful Social Media presence.
- **SocialRank:** Identify, organize, and manage your followers on Twitter.
- **WriteRack:** The best way to tweetstorm.
- **MyTweetLinks:** Increases Twitter traffic.
- **Later:** Easily plan & schedule your Instagram posts.
- **Ritetag:** Instant hashtag analysis.
- **Bitly:** Create, share, and track shortened links.
- **Addthis:** Get more shares, follows and conversions.
- **App Review Monitor:** App reviews delivered to Slack and your inbox.

- **Presskit Generator:** Generate a Press Kit for your iOS App for free.

DESIGN RESOURCES AND INSPIRATION

- **Figma:** Design collaboratively, build prototypes, and leverage best-in-class integrations
- **Freebbble:** High-quality design freebies from Dribbble.
- **Google Fonts:** Free, open-source fonts optimized for the web.
- **The Noun Project:** Thousands of glyph icons from different artists.
- **Premium Pixels:** Free stuff for creatives.
- **Fribbble:** Free PSD resources by Dribbblers curated by Gilbert Pellegrom.
- **SketchAppResources:** Free graphical resources.
- **Squarespace Free Logo:** You can download free low-res version for free.
- **Site Inspire:** Web design inspiration.
- **Land-Book:** Product landing pages gallery.
- **Icon Finder:** Free icon section of the website.

FREE STOCK PHOTOGRAPHY

- **Stock Up:** Best free stock photo websites in one place.
- **Pexels:** Best free photos in one place.
- **All The Free Stock:** Free stock images, icons, and videos.
- **Unsplash:** Free (do whatever you want) high-resolution photos.
- **Startup Stock Photos:** Go. Make something.
- **Super Famous:** Photos by Dutch interaction designer Folkert Gorter.
- **Picography:** Free hi-resolution photos.

145

- **Pixabay:** Free high quality images.

QA AND TESTING

- **Window Resizer:** See how your site looks on various screen resolutions.
- **CrossBrowserTesting:** Test your site on the same browsers and devices your customers use.

DISCOVER TOOLS & STARTUPS

- **Product Hunt:** Curation of the best new products, every day.
- **Launching Next:** Get the best new startups delivered to your inbox daily.
- **Inbound:** Get trending inbound marketing info in your inbox.
- **AngelList:** Where the world meets startups.
- **Beta List:** Discover and get early access to tomorrow's startups.

NEWSLETTERS THAT DON'T SUCK

- **Startup Digest:** Personalized newsletter for all things startup in your area.
- **Tech.co:** A refreshing alternative to TechCrunch.
- **TheSkimm:** An edgy update on what happened in the last 24 hours.

OUTSOURCING

- **Upwork:** Matches professionals and agencies to businesses seeking specialized talent.
- **Guru:** Find and hire talented freelancers for anything.

- **Gun.io:** Find the development help you need. You even get a "Hacker Ambassador" to show you the way.

LEGAL

- **CooleyGo:** Incorporation Packages and other free legal documents:
- **Kiss:** Free legal docs for startup founders and investor.
- **Docracy:** An open collection of free legal documents.
- **Shake:** Create, sign and send legally binding agreements in seconds. Free for personal use.

A4. PRODUCT CASE STUDY: LOCAL LISTINGS

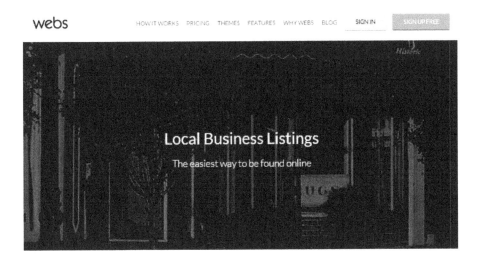

Lessons from a New Product Manager

BUILDING THE ORIGINAL VISTAPRINT LOCAL SEARCH PRODUCT (2009)

Vistaprint Digital built the original local search product in mid-2009 and has sold the product to SMBs since Q4 2009 (October – December 2009). In the pre -build data partner exploration, Localeze was chosen as a data partner for the new product. Infogroup was also considered at the time as a potential data partner.

PRODUCT STRENGTHS

In concept, the Vistaprint Local Search product is incredibly powerful. For a cheap price ($4.99/month) and with relatively little effort (10 minutes), you can submit your key business information to over 100 directories online.

VISTAPRINT LOCAL SEARCH EXTERNAL PAGE

The product is easy to use, affordable, generally intuitive, and has a great marketing message.

VISTAPRINT LOCAL SEARCH INFORMATION FORM

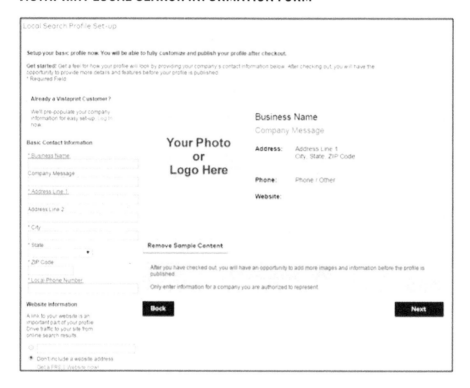

PRODUCT WEAKNESSES

When the Local Search product was first introduced in late 2009, the offering was generally in line with modern web conventions. Today, the product features large amounts of explanatory, but "crowded", text. In addition to the design of the application being out of date, there were several other key weaknesses of the product:

1. DOES THE PRODUCT WORK?

Data aggregators like Localeze, Infogroup, and Acxiom are inherently "black boxes". They rely on directories like Yahoo Local, AOL, YP.com, and others to come to them for data. These directories pick up the data at different frequencies (bi-weekly/monthly) and are allowed to use this data how they wish. Some use most of the data, while others only use bits-and-pieces to construct their databases.

2. SO, WHY IS THIS A SUBSCRIPTION PRODUCT?

The Local Search product that was launched in 2009 is largely cause-and-effect in nature. It's very easy to understand how to submit your information and how to edit your profile (if necessary). However, the on-going monitoring and analytics provided **are minimal at best**.

The current product also **lacks the important ability to identify when a user is listed on a partner directory**. Additionally, the product does not connect to our in-house statistics application to "prove" to users that they are getting additional traffic to their websites from these local directories.

3. PRODUCT SATISFACTION

The Vistaprint Local Search product promises BIG things: "Get Listed on Google" and "Get Listed on 100+ Directories", but **largely fails to deliver** on these promises. Early in the product's lifecycle, this reality was over-ridden by the phenomenal growth and bookings generated by the product. More recently, however, customers have noticed the weaknesses of the product and reviews have been generally negative

The product had an NPS of -32 in the 9/2013 – 6/2014 time period.

USER REVIEWS OF VISTAPRINT LOCAL SEARCH

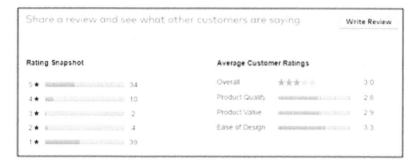

CROSS SELL OF VISTAPRINT LOCAL SEARCH IN WEBSITE CHECKOUT FLOW

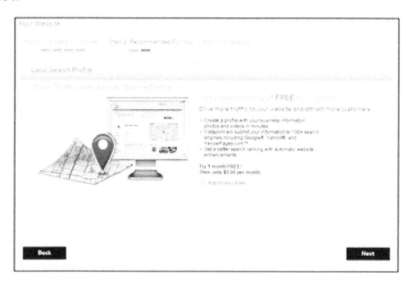

What I Learned: Sometimes great products are diamonds in the rough.

DECISION TO UPDATE LOCAL SEARCH

Since 2011, Local Search has been the **second-highest bookings digital product for Vistaprint** (after Websites). In May 2014, it was decided in Product Quarterly planning that my team at Webs would work on rebuilding the product; first launching it to Webs users, and then migrating it to Vistaprint users with the assistance of another development team.

VP API WORK IN ADVANCE OF PROJECT

In June 2014, Seth, a new hire on a separate development team at Vistaprint started work on the isListed and Profile Submission pieces of the application.

According to Seth, his application:

> *"Provides methods for dealing with local search business services (Google Maps, Facebook, etc.). It provides querying, which returns all of the services that a business is or isn't listed [on]. Whether or not a business is "listed" is subjective since there are different levels of being listed. This service deems a business as being listed if a business is found that matches its name [and zip code]. The local search web service also provides an interface to submit businesses for being listed with all of the various local business services through a third-party service, Localeze."*

Seth spent roughly 1–2 months building a Local Search Web Service with architectural assistance from colleagues with more experience. Throughout his work, Seth worked closely with my development team at Webs to discuss service requirements, testing, architecture, access, and design.

BUSINESS PROFILE (WHAT IS SUBMITTED TO LOCALEZE)

Profile json [edit this section]

```
{
        "id" : "53ce9cd639c9641c5413664f",
        "phone" : "5555555555",
        "fax" : "5555555555",
        "altNumber" : "5555555555",
        "mobileNumber" : "5555555555",
        "contactFirstName" : "John",
        "contactLastName" : "Doe",
        "contactTitle" : "Owner",
        "businessName" : "John's Barber Shop",
        "address" : "100 Main Street",
        "city" : "Small Town",
        "state" : "VA",
        "zip" : "24523",
        "plus4" : "1245",
        "categories" : ["BARBER", "HAIR STYLISTS"],
        "paymentMethod" : ["Visa", "Discover"],
        "url" : "http://www.mysite.com",
        "eMail" : "john@mysite.com",
        "yearOpened" : 1950,
        "hoursOfOperation" : [{
                    "open" : 900,
                    "close" : 1700,
                    "days" : ["Monday", "Tuesday", "Wednesday", "Thursday", "Friday"],
                    "type" : "Hours Open"
            }, {
                    "open" : 900,
                    "close" : 1300,
                    "days" : ["Saturday", "Sunday"],
                    "type" : "Hours Open"
            }
        ],
        "languagesSpoken" : ["EN", "DE"],
        "tagLine" : "We're just around the corner.",
        "logoImage" : "http://www.mysite.com/logo.png"
}
```

It's worth pausing here and acknowledging the **incredibly signifi-cant contributions** that Seth and others made to the Local Search foundation. However, it's also worth noting that Seth works at Vistaprint in Waltham, MA. This is both a different location and a different code-base (C#) than my Webs team in Silver Spring, MD.

The impact of this choice echoed both positively and negatively through the Local Search Epic.

> **What I Learned:** There's no such thing as a free lunch.

MY TEAM AT WEBS TAKES OWNERSHIP

Originally, my development team planned to accept Seth's Local Search Web Service following the completion of their **Internationalization epic**. However, due to product and resource timing, they chose to complete the **Package and Price Restructuring epic** first.

In July 2014, near the end of the Package and Price Restructuring Epic, my team spiked extensively on the Local Search service that Seth and others built. Additionally, my team developed the technical architecture plan for the Webs product. Development on the Local Search MVP began in August 2014.

> **What I Learned:** *I needed to learn more about technical architecture.*

MVP BUILD

In planning for the Local Search MVP Epic, my team estimated that it would take roughly 4 sprints (8 weeks) to take the Local Search Web Service written by Seth and launch an MVP product to Webs users.

There were **several key features required** for the Local Search MVP:

1. **Search My Business:** By submitting a business name and zip code, I should be able to see how many directories I am listed on by querying the "isListed" API service.

2. **Purchase Local Search:** After searching how my business ranks, I should be able to purchase a product from Webs that gives me a Local Search product entitlement.

3. **Complete a Business Information Form:** If I have purchased the Local Search product, I should be able to complete a form that contains all of the important business information I want to submit to Localeze (our data partner).

4. **Submit My Information to Localeze:** Once the form is completed by the Local Search buyer, we needed to connect to the Local Search Web Service to submit this information to Localeze.

5. **Profile Page:** After successful submission, users should have a page where they can see the information they previously submitted to Localeze. Additionally, we should repurpose the lookup services in #1 above to show if a customer is listed on the directories after using the Webs product.

6. **Dashboard Tab for Local Search:** The MVP version of the Webs Local Search product will live on the Webs dashboard (only accessible to Free/Paid Webs users).

My team completed these product features in roughly the 4 sprint (8 week) initial estimate. The MVP was *silently* launched to a 10% of Webs users on the dashboard on Thursday, 10/2/14.

> **What I Learned:** *There's a fine line between MVP and shipping crap.*

What I Learned 2: *It's difficult to determine when a product is ready to launch, but it's the Product Manager's job to explain the value of learning from real users to their team.*

PRE-LAUNCH USERTESTING AND ALPHA TEST

Once my team took ownership of the Local Search product, I sent several emails to current Webs Premium subscribers asking if they would be interested in *"An Exciting New Offering from Webs"* that would help their business *"Get listed in over 100 directories online".*

If users were interested, they were prompted to complete a survey that included most of the information about their business that they would be ultimately be able to submit to Localeze through the Webs Local Search product. Out of the 1,000 users contacted, approximately 50 responded to the survey with detailed information about their business. Out of this population of 50 responses, 30 contained all of the required data to submit a listing to Localeze.

This population helped the team understand some of the **key challenges with the Localeze product** (time to listing, what directories were more/less reliable, etc.) and allowed me to interact with users at an early stage in the build cycle and truly understand the visibility challenges that small business owners experience.

Once the MVP was launched, these users were given promo codes to access the product at a discounted rate. Ideally, I would have liked to have given these users a **free subscription**; however, there were technical limitations that would have required extra work.

> *What I Learned: Get a product to users as fast as possible, even if you're still pulling all the strings behind the scenes.*

PRE-LAUNCH "EARLY BIRD" EMAIL LIST

Throughout the MVP build process, I ran Qualaroo surveys on the Webs dashboard to assess demand and understand pricing.

QUALAROO DEMAND MEASUREMENT SURVEY

In a new tactic for Webs product launches, I **collected emails** from this population that demonstrated interest in the concept ahead of launch. This will be referred to as the "Early Bird" email list. The list reached approximately 3k users in size by 10/2/14.

> *What I Learned: Every launch should include at least 1 thing you've never done before.*

PRE-LAUNCH BLOG POST

While the Local Search product was still being built, I also wrote a blog post on the importance of Local Search for SMBs. The article was intended to build Webs user interest in Local Search and highlight the challenge of manually listing yourself in all of the important directories online.

Pre-Launch Blog Post: Get Found Online With Local Search

What I Learned: Product Managers need to market and promote too.

PRE-LAUNCH INTERNAL TESTING

One of the most successful components of the Local Search epic was the pre-launch internal testing. On 9/24/14, approximately 2 weeks prior to launch, my team brought their computers to the lunch area and invited Webs employees to test out the newest product in the Webs family.

The results of the testing were incredible. Over 30 employees created sample accounts with the tool, searched for businesses they knew, and offered creative (and often painful!) feedback. After the 2 hour internal testing period, we had an additional 50 tickets of work.

Some of these tickets were of course substantially more important than others. While some of the feedback was challenging or scary to hear, it was **incredibly helpful** in showing the team what still had to be done before launch.

> **What I Learned:** *Feedback can be painful, but suck it up and listen for the most painful and most repetitive experiences*

MVP LAUNCH

Following the product launch on 10/2/14, my team closely monitored the user experience. After no errors were discovered, the product was ramped from 10% to 25% early on 10/3/14 and 100% by the end of the day on 10/3/14. In the first outbound launch notification, the "Early Bird" email was sent on 10/9/14 to approximately 3k early opt-ins with a 20% promo code for the product.

The next week, notifications were sent to Paid Subscribers (10/14/14) and Free Users (10/16/14), with each email including a 20% promo code for Local Search.

The product had its PR launch on 10/20/14. The public PR launch included:

Blog Post: Introducing Webs Local Search

SOCIAL PROMOTION

Facebook Cover Photo Takeover: Takeover of the Webs Facebook Cover Photo.

Press Release(s):

http://www.prweb.com/releases/2014/10/prweb12263286.htm

http://thesocialmediamonthly.com/give-local-some-love-foolproof-ways-to-conquer-local-search/

AFFILIATE NETWORK OUTREACH

POST-MVP ANALYTICS

Very quickly after launch, I realized that we weren't tracking enough data on our Local Search buyers. For a product like this, purchases and bookings alone weren't sufficient. Matt, a developer on my team, helped set up a Mixpanel funnel that covered the main steps of the user experience: Landing Page Visit, Search for Business, Shopping Cart, Purchase, and Local Search Profile Submission.

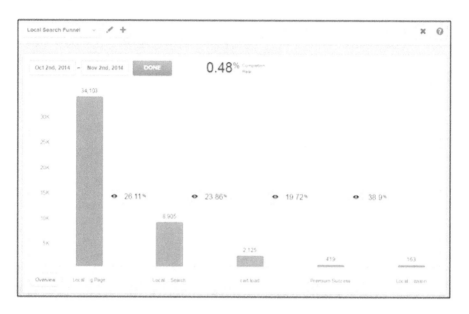

It's common with this type of additional analytics work that you can't see the full value initially. You might even choose not to do the work because the on-paper benefits don't add up: *"Sure, it's interesting to know the conversion rates of each step, but what do they really tell you for a brand-new product (at least on Webs)?"*

Well, with each of these stages, Matt also passed user-inputted data. For example with the business search event in Mixpanel, he passed the business name and zip code entered by the user. Although this was largely an afterthought for Matt and me at the time, **this data turned out to be incredibly valuable.**

In the early days of Webs Local Search, a significant minority of the buyers were non-US. Since the product doesn't work outside of the US, these purchases almost always resulted in refunds. With a quick look at Mixpanel, I was able to see how many users were searching for international addresses.

INTERNATIONAL BUSINESS SEARCHES IN LOCAL LISTINGS

businessName

Sito Pedro

Shiatsu Santé Bordeaux

delhi law firm

Handmade for Heroes, Inc.

Pias Engineers

ISubNow

Samurai Katana Sword Philippines

Based on this analysis, my team made a quick copy update to make it clearer that the product was US only.

Purchase Local Listings »

Please Note: The Local Listings Product is Only for US-Based Businesses

What I Learned: More data and measurement is always better, especially with a new product.

POST-LAUNCH MVP USERTESTING

After the Local Search product launch on Webs, I quickly started UserTesting with www.usertesting.com and ran 5 tests on 10/23/14 and 5 tests on 10/29/14.

THE NPS (NET PROMOTER SCORE) FOR THIS INITIAL ROUND OF USERTESTING ON THE MVP PRODUCT WAS -11.

NPS is calculated as (% of Promoters —% of Detractors). Promoters are defined as scores of 9 and 10, while Detractors are defined as scores of 1–6. While this initial round of UserTesting and our NPS score were somewhat discouraging, it's worth putting the scores into context. The Local Search MVP product had been built in only 8 weeks.

Additionally, the NPS score can be compared to the NPS score of -32 for the Vistaprint Local Search product. Finally, this round of UserTesting was extremely valuable because it exposed the most glaring issues with the Local Search MVP:

1. **The search experience wasn't good:** At the launch of the MVP, our isListed API service could only return if a user was or wasn't listed on Google. Additionally, the user search experience made it seem like we searched many more directories. When a customer was relatively savvy, or knew where their business was listed online, we broke their trust at the first search.

2. **What is 100+ Directories/What Other Directories are Included?** Users were confused exactly where they were being submitted. There wasn't a link to the 100+ Directories so us-

ers were confused if this was the name of the directory or what other directories were included in the 100+.

3. **Submission Errors:** 2 of our 10 test users ran into issues when they submitted their correctly formatted, correctly entered business forms. One of the surprising benefits of user testing was **seeing exactly how users on different browsers, different internet speeds, in different countries experienced errors in the product.**

4. **Challenges with the Category Picker**: Sometimes it's hard to see that a user function is confusing until you actually see a user test it and speak through their thoughts. One of these surprising challenges for our users was selecting categories for their business.

We had a free text form (with no placeholder text) that didn't offer any clear indication that it had search functionality. Most users clicked in the box and then proceeded to try to find their business type in a non-alphabetically sorted list that was almost 2,000 categories long!

Categories *

Search Here For Your Business Category

Please select at least one category and no more than two.

Category Selections Remaining 2

We quickly realized we needed to improve this experience

Category Picker 2.0

> **What I Learned:** *UserTesting/User Simulation is the* **most important thing** *you can do as a Product Manager when you launch a new product.*

MVP NAME TEST

Soon after launching the MVP Local Search product on Webs, I wanted to test the name. The product was getting a substantial amount of clicks per day (2–3k), so volume for the test wouldn't be a concern. The test was simple, test the champion "Local Search" against two competitors: "Local Listings" and "Get Found Online". As is the case for most simple tests at Webs like this, the test was run through the Optimizely testing platform.

The results 2 weeks later were conclusive: **"Local Listings" gets clicked on 11% more**

Quickly, the name was changed to Local Listings. Unfortunately, this backtracking was annoying for the team, but it's the type of test that is difficult to execute prior to launch. Once the migration to Vistaprint is complete, we executed a similar name test.

> **What I Learned:** *Sometimes you need to backtrack to get on the right path*

PHASE II MILESTONES

Following the MVP launch on 10/2, the team took a 2–3 sprint break from the now-named "Local Listings" to focus on building the Webs

Referral program. However, my team immediately started planning for **Local Listings Phase II**, where we would take what we had learned from UserTesting, internal testing, and actual users and decide what features to build next.

After taking into account all of these data input sources, the team began on Phase II Local Listings in the beginning of November 2014. The key priorities for Phase II were:

1. **Improve Stability of the Local Listings Application/Track Errors:** Stability issues in both the development and live environments were causing development challenges and paying user downtime.

2. **Improve Submission Form, Edit Listing:** The submission form, while functional, was in need of several important UX enhancements. Additionally, the team needed to add the functionality to edit a listing, a feature that didn't make it into the initial MVP work.

3. **Launch Improved Business Search:** As the team saw in UserTesting, our business search wasn't great and several things needed to be done to enhance the user experience there.

4. **Add Additional Directories to isListed Service:** At the launch of the MVP, there was only one matching service in isListed for Google. A separate team added Yelp in late October, but 2 directories were still far too few for an effective Local Listings product.

5. **Create an External Presence for Local Listings:** The MVP Local Listings product was only launched to the Webs dashboard. Partly as a merchandising technique, but more importantly as a way to test iFrame-ing elements of the Local Listings application, the team sought to launch the Local Listings application at an external site: Webs Local Listings External Site.

6. **Show Success Sooner:** As we reviewed earlier, one of the biggest complaints with the Vistaprint Local Listings product is that customers really didn't know if it was working. In Phase II, my team truly wanted to **show success sooner.** This included adding a lookup service for Localeze/Neustar, where every customer would be listed instantly and default a green check for 100+ Directories. Following this work, the minimum green checks for any user would be 2. **Success shown instantly.**

7. **Polish + Look Towards VP Migration:** A key element of Phase II work was looking forward towards migration. At each sprint planning meeting, the team considered whether the feature in question was needed by Vistaprint.

Although we wanted to make Webs customers happy, we needed to rationalize that the Vistaprint population was considerably (10–20X/month) larger. This goal resulted in prioritized features like listing logos ahead of adding emails for Webs users.

> **What I Learned:** *Phase II's are exciting. It's where you get to take what you learned from real users and put work against it.*

STABILITY ISSUES (THANKSGIVING 2014)

Thanksgiving 2014 was not kind to the nascent Local Listings application. Over the period of the 4 day holiday, Local Listings was down for a collective 48 hours. There were several key stability issues that caused downtime in the Local Listings application:

1. Networking Issues with Vistaprint Servers
2. oAuth Authentication
3. Server Load Balancer
4. API Code Errors (ex. API could be broken by user)
5. MongoDB Connection Errors

> **What I Learned:** *Stability isn't sexy. But downtime is even uglier.*

DIRECTORIES ADDED

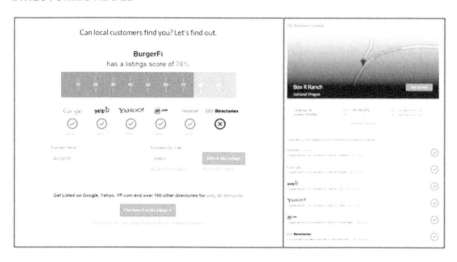

One of the main goals of Local Listings Phase II was to add more directories to the search and profile pages. My team delivered strongly on this mission, **launching services for Neustar/Localeze, YP.com, and Yahoo** over the 2014 holiday season.

> **What I Learned:** *Shower your users with success and they'll stick around*

PAID SEARCH

After the initial "Local Search" external page (www.webs.com/features/local-search) was launched in late November 2014, I wanted to experiment with pushing more traffic there. At the time, the external page was receiving a minimal amount of traffic from organic keywords like "Business Listing" and "Business Directory". In the first week of December, Webs began a small scale paid search campaign targeting these types of search queries on Google.

Initially, the results weren't too great. The cost of the keywords was approximately 50% more than the LTV (Lifetime Value) of the Local Search buyers. However, there were improvements to be made.

For the first 3 weeks of the paid search campaign, the Local Search/Local Listings external page still featured the "old v1" search experience. In late December 2014, this was replaced by the iFrame experience above. Since the new experience was launched in late

December, approximately 396 visitors have come from CPC sources at a cost of ~$2/click.

From these 396 visitors, there were 7 Local Listings buyers with a total LTV of $1,182 in the first week.

> **What I Learned:** *Learn why something isn't working. Fix it. Measure the results.*

CONTINUED USERTESTING

UserTesting was an integral part of the Local Listings product development from MVP through the completion of Phase II. Although UserTesting.com testers were non-Webs users, they still were small businesses that could comment effectively on the Webs Local Listings product.

From October 2014 to early-January 2015, I ran UserTesting.com tests with 23 different users. Each of these ~30 minute sessions provided a wealth of information that helped me prioritize backlog items, identify errors, and improve poor user experiences. As we discussed earlier, the Webs Local Search product began with an NPS of -11 in October 2014. However, after a significant portion of the Phase II improvements, 4/5 users tested on 1/9/14 were "Promoters", while the 5th tester responded to the NPS question with an 8/10 score.

> **What I Learned:** *UserTesting is great. When you see improvements based on your work, it's incredible.*

LIVE USER FEEDBACK — QUALAROO

In addition to the UserTesting through www.usertesting.com, my team implemented Qualaroo within the Local Listings application to get real-time NPS data from actual Local Listings buyers. If a user is a "Detractor", a follow-up question provides a free-response input for why they are not likely to recommend. If a user is a "Promoter", a follow-up question nudges a user towards providing a testimonial, which we would like to use on our product in the future.

Additionally, as an "unexpected benefit" of Qualaroo in our application, we've been able to **offer targeted promo codes to users**. For example, if a user is about to abandon the business search page after being there for 30 seconds, we can popup a promo code offer and try to retain them.

> **What I Learned:** *Qualaroo can serve many purposes for a new product and can target customers incredibly well.*

2015 WRAP-UP

As the team entered 2015, we were excited to wrap up the goals of Phase II still outstanding, as well as some new ones that had surfaced as they thought about VP migration:

1. **Build a Webs isListed Service**: Bundle the individual services into a maintainable, extendable, and understandable API that can be called by both Webs and Vistaprint.

2. **Add Statistics to Local Listings:** In a further effort to show Local Listings users that the product is working, we'll expose pageviews from Local sources.

3. **Upload Photo/Logo With Business Listing**: A significant portion of Vistaprint Website/Local Search users have a logo for their business. In mid-January 2015, the team added this feature to the business information form.

4. **Add Facebook to isListed**: As the team neared the end of Local Listings, they added Facebook as another directory on the isListed API.

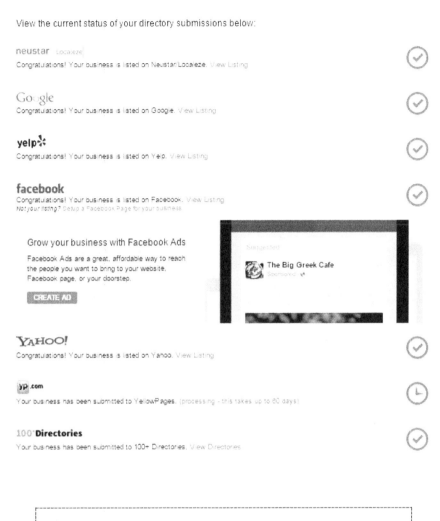

> **What I Learned:** *Once you've built momentum, it's tough to stop building.*

DATA PARTNER EVALUATION

In late 2014 and early 2015, we also explored additional data partners that could improve on the submission and listings aspects of the Local Listings product. While Localeze is cheap, it is a black box and offers no guarantee a user will be listed. Additionally, our team had to research on our own to determine what directories were the most likely for our users to get listed on.

Landscape of Data Partners

	Localeze	Yext	Acxiom	InfoGroup	Factual
Cost Structure	$1.33/ Submission	$3/$8/$15 per month in perpetuity	$8/listing per year ---------- $3/listing per year	$7/listing per year ---------- $5/listing per year	Free
Volume	$100k/yr.	TBD	25-50k --------- 50-75k upfront & 4k/month	50k --------- 100k	Free
Pros	• Cost Structure is amazing • Relationship already in place	• Get Listed "instantly" • Dashboard infrastructure	• Higher Quality Data Partner	• Higher Quality Data Partner • Foundational Data Set • More experience in navigation • Quicker listing on Yahoo/WP/Citysearch	• It's free • Moz uses it, so it probably is worth checking out
Cons	• Black Box • Long update times (directories pick up data on monthly basis) • Not much support	• Price makes no sense on low-end • How would cost structure change with Yext as upsell only?	• Still a black box like Localeze • Long update times (directories pick up data on monthly basis)	• Still a black box like Localeze • Long update times (directories pick up data on different time periods)	• No support • Still a black box with long times between submission and appearance
Other Details					http://developer.factual.com/write-api/
Contact	Joel.smart@neustar.biz	cward@yext.com	Travis.norris@acxiom.com	Joe.lazure@infogroup.com	n/a

After evaluating these data partners, the team decided to continue to use Localeze for our base offering and conduct demand testing to explore a higher end, DIFY solution in early 2015. If there is appetite at a higher price point for a more robust product, we plan to explore a partnership with Yext.

What I Learned: *You generally get what you pay for with data partners.*

MIGRATION TO VISTAPRINT

An expanded team migrated the Local Listings product from Webs to Vistaprint to replace the legacy Local Search product in 2015.

1. **Launch New External Page**
2. **Replace Local Search Product** with Webs Local Listings Product via iFrame
3. **Price/Name/Merchandising Testing**

LOCAL LISTINGS MARKETING VIDEOS

With the Local Listings videos, George, Webs' videographer, wanted to depart from the typical feature-based videos that Webs and Vistaprint were known for. Instead, they wanted to highlight the problem of missing/incorrect listings to business owners in an engaging, realistic, and humorous way.

1. Piano/Music Teacher
2. Locksmith
3. Florist

GREAT DECISIONS IN LOCAL LISTINGS EPIC

1. **Internal and UserTesting**: If you're not doing these as a Product Manager, you're not doing your job.

2. **Launch strategy:** Have a diverse launch strategy because you don't know what channel will resonate strongest with your customers.

3. **"Show Success Sooner"**: Make sure customers feel like they are getting what they pay for and make that feeling happen as quickly as possible.

4. **Spending a lot of time with users:** Beyond internal and external testing, you should be simulating, emailing, and surveying your users consistently.

POOR DECISIONS IN LOCAL LISTINGS EPIC

1. Having someone at a different location, on a different team, with a different schedule, create a vital service that our application relies on.
2. I should have brought a key member or two from the team to Vistaprint to meet the individuals responsible for the application architecture.
3. Architecture and Stability are **IMPORTANT!**
4. Error monitoring should be set up before errors occur, not after.

CASE QUESTIONS

1. What would you have done differently than Alex and the development team for the Local Listings product?
2. What decisions made by Alex did you most agree with? Where do you think he should have been more involved or less involved?
3. Where do you see the future of the Local Listings product? What opportunities does the product have that Alex may have missed?
4. Which of Alex's learning's was most significant to you and why?
5. Would you have released sooner than Alex? Later? Why?

A5. PRODUCT DEVELOPMENT TIMELINE

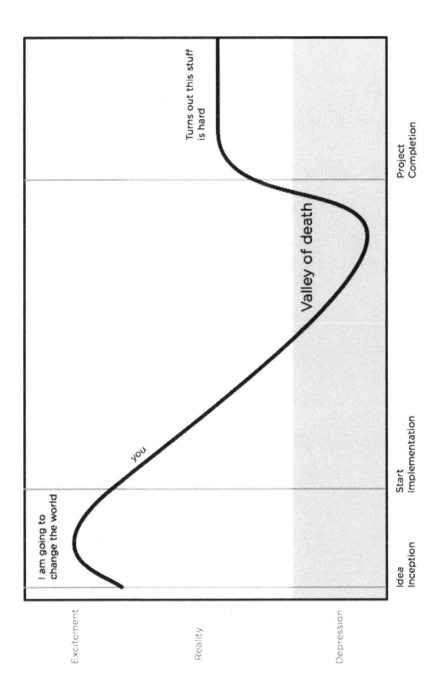

ABOUT THE AUTHOR

Alex wrote Building Digital Products to help the new Product Manager who feels in way over their head, the experienced Product Manager looking to step up his or her game, and the expert Product Manager who understands that there is always more to learn.

Alex is also the author of Disrupting Yourself, which he wrote to help others by sharing the tips and tricks that have helped him to consistently level up throughout his career. Alex is the author of a technology blog on Medium that has over 1 million annual readers.

Currently, Alex works for ICX Media as the Chief Product Officer and Bullseye as a Founding Advisor. ICX Media helps Media Companies, Brands, and Agencies leverage Data Inspired Storytelling. Bullseye helps level the playing field for College Admissions.

Before ICX Media, Alex spent close to 2 years as a Director of Product at Upside Travel, a technology startup that has reinvented booking business travel for companies with less than 500 employees.

Previous to Upside Travel, Alex worked for Vistaprint Digital for 4 years, largely in Product Management, managing the Identity Family of Products, totaling more than $50MM in revenue.

Alex is passionate about creating and scaling powerful web and mobile products that make a significant impact in millions of people's lives around the world. Alex deeply enjoys building and managing the product and development teams that help achieve that goal.

Find out more about Alex at www.alexmitchell.co

Made in the USA
Las Vegas, NV
08 December 2021